CW00347330

Palgrave Advances in Bioeconomy: Economics and Policies

Series Editor
Justus Wesseler
Agricultural Economics and Rural Policy Group
Wageningen University
Wageningen, Gelderland, The Netherlands

More information about this series at
http://www.palgrave.com/gp/series/16141

Chris Giotitsas

Open Source Agriculture

Grassroots Technology in the Digital Era

Chris Giotitsas
Ragnar Nurkse Department of Innovation
and Governance
Tallinn University of Technology
Tallinn, Estonia

P2P Lab
Ioannina, Greece

ISSN 2524-5848   ISSN 2524-5856   (electronic)
Palgrave Advances in Bioeconomy: Economics and Policies
ISBN 978-3-030-29340-6   ISBN 978-3-030-29341-3   (eBook)
https://doi.org/10.1007/978-3-030-29341-3

This Palgrave Pivot imprint is published by the registered company Springer Nature
Switzerland AG.
The registered company address is: Gewerbestrasse 11, 6330 Cham, Switzerland

ACKNOWLEDGEMENTS

I wish to thank all the participants of this research who graciously allowed me to join them in their fascinating activities and took time off their busy schedules to offer valuable insight and genuine hospitality. It is my greatest concern to provide an accurate account of their experience and values. More specifically, I wish to thank Julien Reynier and Dorn Cox for their thoughtful guidance before and during my field work in France and the US respectively.

I also wish to thank my P2P Lab family, and especially Vasilis Kostakis, for their love, support and inspiring work all these years.

I acknowledge funding from the School of Business (University of Leicester) as part of the PhD programme and financial support from the European Research Council (ERC) under the European Union's Horizon 2020 research and innovation programme (grant agreement No. 802512).

CONTENTS

CHAPTER 1

Introduction

Abstract This introductory chapter offers the author's motivation for writing this book and sets the framework with which he set about doing his research after he offers a brief account on the evolution and state of commercial agriculture today within the capitalist mode of production. It provides a definition for the concept of open source agriculture and how it is viewed as both a social movement and a technology development model within the context of this book.

Keywords Open source agriculture • Social movement • Technology

I have spent most of my life (so far) in and around a farm in one of the most remote and poor areas of Greece. Being surrounded by farmers and people working in the primary and basic construction sector, I had not appreciated the ingenuity and collaborative effort these people put in their day to day activities to achieve sustainability. It was not until I spent several years away from my family home that it dawned on me how uncritically immersed urbanised societies were in the technology they are handed.

I had always been enamoured with information and communication technologies. I was experimenting with free and open source software and tinkering with hardware to get my work done affordably and to have

© The Author(s) 2019   1
C. Giotitsas, *Open Source Agriculture*, Palgrave Advances in
Bioeconomy: Economics and Policies,
https://doi.org/10.1007/978-3-030-29341-3_1

some control over the digital technologies I have been using. But I came to understand that open source is something beyond an efficient approach to hi-tech. It is a social movement.

Openness, sharing resources and other terms like these are used today to add a "sexiness" factor to products or institutions that do not deserve the name. This has led to the term "openwashing" (borrowed from "greenwashing") to call out this trend. Similarly, participatory or user-driven design, co-creation or co-construction and other concepts have been proposed to include the public or at least some diversity of stakeholders in the technology development. However, such initiatives, mostly externally driven, are often organised top-down and do not essentially involve citizens. Hence, the dichotomy is maintained between expert and layman ignoring the social complexities of stakeholder engagement.

This book explores those initiatives that have been self-mobilised from within farmer communities, in a bottom-up fashion, and are engaging in technology development for the community itself. The practical lessons learned from this research project are being applied in our efforts to provide the local community, where I grew up, with the tools to formulate an effective organisation similar to the ones I discuss here.

This book explores technology designed and produced by farmers to accommodate their particular needs. I trace the emergence of a new social movement that facilitates and promotes this type of technology. I thus discuss two case studies of social movement organisations and their technological communities: the Farm Hack network in the USA and the L'Atelier Paysan initiative in France. The focus is on how they frame their activities and how this translates in the alternative technology development model. I use the following conceptual tools: framing analysis and resource mobilisation theory from the social movement research field, and the constructivist approach and critical theory of technology from the technology research field.

This book illustrates how individuals refuse to embrace a technological system of mainstream agriculture that does not reflect their values and interests, and instead rely on alternative framings of technological culture to give meaning to their vision of how agriculture should be. By doing so, I address a novel collaborative mode of technology production, substantially different from the dominant market-driven one.

I employ the concept of the social movement to describe this collective activity, albeit in an early stage. This enables the tracing of the various ideological frames that contribute to the creation of a common set of principles and goals for those engaging in this activity as well as their efforts to gain support. That is why framing analysis has been selected as a key theoretical approach, combined with an investigation of the incentivising and resource management processes within the movement organisations.

I also examine the details of the production process in the broader sociotechnical environment. I argue that this emerging mode of production signals a break from the capitalist mode of technology production and formulates a more democratised alternative.

1.1 TECHNOLOGY AND CONVENTIONAL AGRICULTURE

The shift from feudalism to capitalism and the start of the land enclosures along with colonialism marked the transformation of agricultural production. The capitalist system evolved alongside agricultural activity, influencing how production took place and, thus, marking a gradual shift from subsistence to commodity production (Brenner 1976; Albritton 1993). While peasants were transformed into labour workers to feed the industrial revolution, machinery and modernised farming techniques, which increased productivity and yields, were introduced to feed. All economic activity became driven by capital accumulation, labour exploitation and escalating competition (Wood 1998). This sparked the accumulation of land and great centralisation of production in large farms, where former peasants became waged labourers (Federici 2004). The capitalist production took not only land from peasants but also the soil itself, meaning the fertility of the land due to overproduction, initiating the need for modern farming methods (Marx 1999).

The competitive environment substantially transformed agriculture and enabled the rise of "agribusiness" (Davis and Goldberg 1957). This term was introduced in 1957 to characterise the infiltration of the industrial sector in agriculture. Intensive industrial agriculture and proprietary technology captured more and more traditional practices from farmers, initially with mechanical inputs that favoured large-scale production (Gifford 1992) and later with chemical and biological ones (Lewontin 1998). This led to the cannibalisation of farms by competitors, who were more adept at the "technology treadmill" (Cochrane 1993), and to the massive expansion of the agribusiness sector. The industries introduced large, complex and expensive motorised machinery that multiplied productivity. The treadmill was initiated and farms were forced to keep upgrading into new inputs to be able to compete (Mazoyer and Roudart 2006). The process of capturing expanded into new methods of farming with the introduction of chemical fertilisers, pesticides and growth hormones but also proprietary, genetically modified seeds, replacing free knowledge and techniques developed and tested by farmers over centuries.

Capitalist accumulation takes place through exclusionary intellectual property licenses and the creation of artificial scarcity. This is justified with the claim that intellectual property rights create incentives for economic agents to pursue the research and development of new products and services (Arrow 1962). Intellectual property in agriculture is manifested in all stages and dominates over farmer-developed options. For instance, patents for plants were issued and the International Union for the Protection of New Varieties of Plants (UPOV) was established. Traditional farmer varieties failed to meet the criteria for protection and over the years were replaced by proprietary ones. The advances in bioengineering in the 1990s spread intellectual property licences drastically (Lewontin 1998), enforcing restrictions not only in specific plants but also in certain traits, genes and even methods that were manufactured in labs (Aoki 2009).

The outcome of this enclosure process has been the tremendous agriculture-related technological concentration in the hands of a few mega-corporations. According to a report (2013) by the ECT (Erosion, Technology and Concentration) group, the world's top three companies control 53% of the global commercial seed market and the top ten control 76% (meaning the seeds that are sold which excludes seeds developed and exchanged by farmers). Moreover, six companies account for 76% of the global agrochemical market; ten pesticide firms hold about 95% of the global market; ten firms control 41% of the global fertiliser market; three companies account for 46% of the animal pharmaceuticals market and seven firms control 72%. Finally, four companies account for 97% of poultry genetics, and another four account for 66% of swine genetics. As far as mechanical inputs are concerned, concentration is continually rising with four companies controlling 50% of the global market by 2009 and eight companies controlling more than 60% (Fuglie et al. 2011). Meanwhile, by 2008 five companies held 90% of the global grain trade, three countries produced 70% of maize and the 30 largest food retailers accounted for 33% of world grocery sales (McMichael 2009).

The starting points for oppositional activities have been at least two. First, the notion that conventional agriculture presents severe challenges to small-scale farmers. Second, the technology model supporting it has removed the farmers from the creative process of developing artefacts supposed to accommodate their activity, largely ignoring their empirical input and desires.

Mumford (1964) claimed that there are two parallel sets of technology: one authoritarian and one democratic. The former is system-centred and powerful but also unstable. It is centralised, large-scale and with a high degree of specialisation that turns humans into resources. While this system has been around for centuries, it has infiltrated modern society to such a degree because it seemingly accepts the basic principle of democracy. Its products are equally available to anyone who can afford them. However, one can only take what the system offers. The latter set is human-centred, based in craft and agricultural communities whose activity is, while limited, adaptable and durable. This type of technology, characterised by creativity and autonomy, is developed to address specific social needs through appropriate means.

Such a distinction, simplistic and wide open to criticism as it may be, builds a framework to explore the potentialities of an alternative technological strand. I look into initiatives that formulate a new social movement; whose goal is to promote open source technology developed by its users in agriculture against the perceived authoritarian version of the agricultural system. I thus examine the political, economic, ethical and cultural stimuli behind their technological development as opposed to the economic-political agenda of the agribusiness sector.

1.2   Conceptualising Open Source Agriculture as a New Social Movement

I study initiatives that consist of small-scale and organic farmers, adherent designers and engineers, and activists, who oppose the socioeconomic and technological aspects of conventional agricultural production but also its other, more severe, consequences. For instance, its environmental impact due to the large-scale methods employed and the reliance on fossil fuel resources (Tilman 1999); the significant reduction of biodiversity (Biao et al. 2003); the great increase in energy requirements (La Rosa et al. 2008) and the depletion and contamination of water (Brown 2004). These open source initiatives are collaboratively designing and manufacturing their tools and machines to address their needs. Using modern information and communication technologies (hereafter ICT), the designs for these pieces of technology are made available for anyone to adopt and adapt to their needs.

This activity, which I call open source agriculture, is discussed in the context of an emerging social movement, and it is the primary focus of this book. This treatment allows me to make sense of the breadth of factors that affect the development process as well as their output. Because if we are to call the aggregation of initiatives producing open source technology for agriculture an emerging social movement, then we may contextualise it within social movements that came before it. That is to locate commonalities and trace linkages as well as the values and ethics they embody in a structured way. It also allows the investigation of initiatives as social movement organisations, which seek to secure and distribute resources necessary for their operational activity, as well as provide adherents with incentives that correspond to their specific interests and values to elicit participation. I explore the creative capacity of the movement that goes beyond opposition and the organisational particularities that facilitate it, focusing on the technology development processes.

1.3   Formulating a Technology Development Model from within the Movement

This new social movement is identified as technology-oriented with the focus placed on the mode of technology production that emerges from within its activity. When reviewing the progress of technology on a grander scale, the complexity of the issue makes discerning a pattern that clearly explains the evolution of technological development tricky. Instead, we should look back in history to establish what social circumstances lead to certain technological outcomes. For instance, the fall of the guild system at the end of the eighteenth century and the rise and struggle to maintain control in capitalist production is what defines the conditions for technological development until today (Feenberg 2002). While the change looks quantitative and technical at first look, a profound qualitative change, which was a necessary condition for industrialisation, also took place in work, design, management and conditions with the main feature being the deskilling of workers (Ibid.). If guilds had managed, instead, to evolve into worker-driven manufacturing facilities, the nature of technological development would have been different.

The transition to the capitalist economic system of production brought about a radical change in the way technology is developed by transferring control from the craftsman to the owners of productive resources and managers (Feenberg 2010a). Technical values, experience gained and lessons learned from using technologic artefacts were no longer feeding back into the development of technology. While the technology expert and the user would interact closely before, in capitalist production, their connection has been largely severed (Feenberg 2010b). Therefore, the consequences that escaped the scope of profit from newly developed technology became irrelevant.

Herbert Marcuse criticised the technological rationality developed by technoscientific management that proliferates in capitalism despite its apparent irrationalities (Marcuse 1970). This rings true in the agricultural context, where industrialisation has had an enormous impact. These irrationalities are the starting point for critique, which, if followed by the establishment of a new historical subject (a vague notion understood as a catalyst or agent), may progressively, despite limitations, lead to transformation (Marcuse 1970).

Due to its characteristics, peer-produced open source technology, as presented in the following chapters, could form such a subject pushing for technology that breaks free from the capitalist framework. It presents a possible bottom-up alternative for citizen inclusion in the development process of technology. An alternative that goes beyond the arguably suspicious populist appropriation of the language of "participation" from the political and scientific elites (Thorpe 2008; Levidow 2007). Open source technology can be viewed as subject to reconstruction and democratic participation, enabling people "to participate effectively in a widening range of public activities" (Feenberg 2002, p.3). It also echoes Gorz's (1983) argument that decentralised productive infrastructures, focusing on the development of locally controlled technologies, are vital for democratising decision-making.

In this vein, I use as a starting point those independent initiatives that already engage individuals in the co-creation of technological artefacts. Their experience can, potentially, provide valuable insight in the theorising of democratisation of technology in general and "socially inclusive", "participant driven", "grassroots" development more specifically rather than attempting to explore this activity through conventional top-down means and institutions.

Up to this point, the development process of open source technology has been researched marginally. Most available studies have focused on the characteristics and development models of open source software. This book uses these theoretical approaches to formulate a robust theoretical and practical underpinning for technology development. The collective framing within the movement provides the foundation for the technologic development process and artefacts produced. The goal is not only to understand the process through which this technology is produced, regarding the interests or goals of those involved, but also to look at the effect of the broader economic and cultural factors.

1.4   BOOK STRUCTURE

Chapter 2 presents the research methodology as well as the data gathering and analysis processes for the book. I outline the methods used to gather, process and present my data. Hence, the readers not interested in methods may skip this chapter.

Chapter 3 reviews the relevant social movement theories focusing on the resource mobilisation and the framing theories, used in this book. Of interest is the role of social movement organisations and selective incentives for participation in social movements since material artefacts are developed as part of the movement activity examined here. The framing activities that social movements engage in are pertinent in the context of wider master frames.

Chapter 4 examines the master frames identified as the main contributors to the creation of the open source agriculture movement. Specifically, the organic, peasant and open source frames are synthesised to understand what motivates the adherents of the movement to engage in the production of technological artefacts. Moreover, I review both social movement organisations through the resource mobilisation viewpoint and examine the material factors affecting this process.

Chapter 5 discusses the technology theory applied in the book. I emphasise the technological frames as tools of the social constructivism of technology school of thought and the application of the social movement analysis output in the technological analysis. Emphasis is also placed on the critical theory of technology that provides a normative perspective in technological development emerging from the juxtaposition of the technological actors and modern large-scale agribusiness.

Chapter 6 addresses the two cases, this time under the technology theory lens. Firstly, I explore the various aspects of activity, such as their organisational and economic models formulated to support technological development. Secondly, I apply social construction and critical perspectives to study the technological development process in the micro and macro level, respectively.

Chapter 7 provides a vision for an alternative technological rationale emanating from this and other technological social movements. I argue why and how this emerging mode of production should and could expand globally.

BIBLIOGRAPHY

Albritton, B. (1993) "Did Agrarian Capitalism Exist?", *The Journal of Peasant Studies*, 20(3), pp. 419–441

Aoki, K. (2009) "'Free Seeds, Not Free Beer': Participatory Plant Breeding, Open Source Seeds, and Acknowledging User Innovation in Agriculture", *Fordham Law Review*, 77, pp. 2276–2310

Arrow, K. (1962) "Economic Welfare and the Allocation of Resources for Invention", in Arrow, K. (ed) *The Rate and Direction of Inventive Activity: Economic and Social Factors*, Princeton, NJ: Princeton University Press, pp. 609–625

Biao, X., Xiaorong, W., Zhuhong, D. and Yaping, Y. (2003) "Critical Impact Assessment of Organic Agriculture", *Journal of Agricultural and Environmental Ethics*, 16(3), pp. 297–311

Brenner, R. (1976) "Agrarian Class Structure and Economic Development in Pre-Industrial Europe", *Past & Present*, 70, pp. 30–75

Brown, L. (2004) *Outgrowing the Earth, the Food Security Challenge in an Age of Falling Water Tables and Rising Temperatures*, New York: W.W. Norton

Cochrane, W.W. (1993) *The Development of American Agriculture: A Historical Analysis*, Minneapolis: University of Minnesota Press

Davis, J.H. and Goldberg, R.A. (1957) *A Concept of Agribusiness*, Boston: Division of Research, Graduate School of Business Administration, Harvard University

ECT Group. (2013) "Putting the Cartel before the Horse...Who Will Control Agricultural Inputs?", Available at: http://www.etcgroup.org/sites/www.etc-group.org/files/Communique%CC%81%20111%204%20sep%203%20pm.pdf, accessed 18 March 2016

Federici, S. (2004) *Caliban and the Witch: Women, the Body and Primitive Accumulation*, Brooklyn, NY: Autonomedia

Feenberg, A. (2002) *Transforming Technology: A Critical Theory Revisited*, New York: Oxford University Press

Feenberg, A. (2010a) "Ten Paradoxes of Technology", *Techne*, 14(1), pp. 3–15
Feenberg, A. (2010b) *Between Reason and Experience*, Cambridge, MA: MIT Press
Fuglie, K.O., Heisey, P.W., King, J.L., Pray, C.E., Day-Rubenstein, K., Schimmelpfennig, David, Wang, S. Ling and Karmarkar-Deshmukh, R. (2011) "Research Investments and Market Structure in the Food Processing, Agricultural Input, and Biofuel Industries Worldwide", *ERR-130. U.S. Department of Agriculture, Economic Research Service*
Gifford, R.C. (1992) *Agricultural Engineering in Development: Concepts and Principles*, Food & Agriculture Organization
Gorz, A. (1983) *Ecology as Politics*, London: Pluto
La Rosa, A.D., Siracusa, G. and Cavallaro, R. (2008) "Energy Evaluation of Sicilian Red Orange Production. A Comparison between Organic and Conventional Farming", *Journal of Cleaner Production*, 16, pp. 1907–1915
Levidow L. (2007) "European Public Participation as Risk Governance: Enhancing Democratic Accountability for Agbiotech Policy?", *East Asian Science, Technology and Society: An International Journal*, 1(1), pp. 19–51
Lewontin, R.C. (1998) "The Maturing of Capitalist Agriculture: Farmer as Proletarian", *Monthly Review*, 50(3), pp. 72–84
Marcuse, H. (1970) *Five Lectures*, Beacon
Marx, K. (1999) "Capital: A Critique of Political Economy, Volume I", Available at: https://www.marxists.org/archive/marx/works/1867-c1/
Mazoyer, M. and Roudart, L. (2006) *A History of World Agriculture*, Routledge
McMichael, P. (2009) "The World Food Crisis in Historical Perspective", *Monthly Review*, 61(3), p. 32
Mumford, L. (1964) "Authoritarian and Democratic Technics", *Technology and Culture*, 5, pp. 1–8
Thorpe, C. (2008) "Political Theory in Science and Technology Studies", in Hackett, EJ, Amsterdamska, O, Lynch, M, Wajcman, J (eds) *The Handbook of Science and Technology Studies*, 3rd edition, Cambridge, MA: MIT Press, pp. 63–82
Tilman, D. (1999) "Global Environmental Impacts of Agricultural Expansion: The Need for Sustainable and Efficient Practices", *PNAS*, 96(11), pp. 5995–6000
Wood, E.M. (1998) "The Agrarian Origins of Capitalism", *Monthly Review, An Independent Socialist Magazine*

CHAPTER 2

How I Researched This

Abstract This brief chapter expands on the methodology devised for this research project, its specificities and limitations. It also discusses how diverse sets of data were collected, examined and presented. It then sets the blueprint for how the rest of the book is structured according to the two theoretical lenses adopted. Namely, social movement theory and technology studies approaches which are used to synthesise a way to explore different sets of value in alternative technological trajectories.

Keywords Research design • Embedded case study • Data analysis

I discuss open source technology development as an alternative technology built on an alternative set of values. To explore how this technological trajectory can manifest, I focus on agriculture by borrowing a social movement theory approach and applying it on technology theories. I, thus, identify the political identity and collective action plan, formulated through the values, goals and interests of the open source agriculture movement. Meaning the aggregation of individuals, organisations and communities, mostly comprised of farmers, who contribute to the development of machines and tools for farming. The design and know-how of these tools are made freely available without restrictions preventing their reproduction. Such activity takes place in various productive fields, yet its

© The Author(s) 2019
C. Giotitsas, *Open Source Agriculture*, Palgrave Advances in
Bioeconomy: Economics and Policies,
https://doi.org/10.1007/978-3-030-29341-3_2

application in this open source agriculture movement provides one of the most mature instances of open source technology besides software.

An embedded case study approach has been adopted to gather and analyse empirical data, to examine individual cases separately but also as part of a larger case. Therefore, the overarching case, open source agriculture, is examined through two subunits of analysis, which provide diverse data for the analysis of the main case (Yin 2003). Engaging in purposive sampling and specifically criterion sampling (Palys and Atchison 2008), the cases I chose are non-profit social movement organisations and their respective communities. Those are L'Atelier Paysan, a cooperative in France that is developing farmer-driven technologies and practices, and Farm Hack, a community of farmers promoting open source tools and machinery designed and developed following the open source principles, in the USA.

Out of the various actors in this movement, these have been selected due to the collaborative and self-mobilised nature of tool development within their rather large communities. Meaning projects that have been initiated by those within farming communities with a goal to develop and disseminate technological solutions that would primarily benefit the community. Initiatives by external organisations like state agencies, research institutions and social enterprises were reviewed but rejected on that basis. That is not to suggest that such projects could not qualify as important for this type of research project. But merely to provide some focus for this book.

Furthermore, I focus on the European and USA regions, mostly due to resource limitations. That does not mean that there are no noteworthy projects in other regions. For instance, the Honey bee network in India, a project initiated by a researcher rather than self-mobilised, promotes technology for poor rural areas that would, potentially, fit in the context of the book. While similarities with the projects selected are significant, each is defined by a unique mixture of local economic, political and cultural characteristics shaping their actions, goals, values and interests. In this regard, beside practical reasons, those two cases were selected to limit the scope of the book even further into the "western world" and allow for an in-depth as well as comparative examination of the selected cases. No doubt further research that would include initiatives from non-western countries would provide much richer insight in the phenomenon studied.

I have managed to secure access through key individuals from both cases which should be viewed mostly as key informants and not as gatekeepers, since despite their varying organisational structures, this type of initiatives avoid rigid hierarchical structures and instead adopt a consensus-driven decision-making system based on mutual validation and meritocracy. This bottom-up approach has previously been described as peer governance (Bauwens 2005). Therefore, these first contacts function primarily as conduits to the rest of the members of each case as well as for further information regarding field work.

2.1   How I Collected Data

I conducted semi-structured interviews with members from each case. Further participant observation was employed, where interaction with members of each case took place on-site to immerse myself and attain a clearer picture of the internal structure and processes of the groups observed. Prominent members within these cases have been identified during the observations and targeted for interviews, while more were secured through snowballing. The latter aimed for those with long standing participation in the organisations and/or particularly interesting perspectives in the context of this book.

The interviews were structured around specific core questions and probes that attempted to elicit important data regarding their goals, desires and ideologies as well as their coordination and development methods. These, in practice, were mostly indicative however and were used to place emphasis on the questions that were deemed most relevant during the design process of this research project. Some topics were of more interest than others to interviewees so they elaborated as they pleased, revealing more interesting questions which I had not previously considered. Furthermore, some interviews took place on site so the surroundings coloured the flow of the discussion.

A detailed list of the interviewees whose names have not been anonymised can be found in the appendix. In fact, none of the people I spoke to had any desire to be anonymous. This whole book is about open access to information and knowledge after all. They even signed a relevant form when the interviews took place as part of my PhD work. However, to have this work published as a book required a second round of (more demanding) consent forms signed, as well as several other forms for the pictures I took during data gathering (which include not only people but also things). Given the fact that many of the interviewees are farmers and not easy to reach as well as the potential and obvious ideological clash means that the visual material had to be removed and some of the respondents anonymised. The irony, of course, is not lost on me but let that be a further comment on how the current socio-economic system treats access to information.

Field observations took place in various sites, including workshops, events and organisation bases of the cases. During those I managed to witness the groups' interactions and activities as well as interact with them. I travelled in France in various occasions during the spring and summer of 2016. There, I participated in two machine prototyping workshops, attended a three-day gathering/festival and spent some time in the operational base of the organisation. The USA case field work took place over a two-week period in various locations in the states of New York, Vermont, New Hampshire and Massachusetts in December 2016. In this trip, I visited farms, attended a prototyping workshop and a farmer tool summit sponsored by the organisation under examination.

In both cases, I had the opportunity to converse with numerous farmers and other individuals involved in the movement as well as observe (and sometimes assist with) the work and general interaction around tool development. On some occasions, I had the privilege to be invited into their homes and share food and stories. Even so, a large part of the activity in this type of initiatives is distributed with their community members widely dispersed in their respective regions (as well as internationally) with much taking place online.

Last, I gathered data from the online platforms, fora, discussion sections and documentation (audio-visual material, reports, articles, blog posts) available as well as email communications with individuals from each case. Given the fact that openness is a principle permeating such initiatives, there are rich and diverse sources available for the mining of research data. Like the interviews, key documents and discussions have been selected that provide the most insight in each case. In other words, those that provided details on the intricacies of the technology development model as well as insight on what motivates participants.

2.2   How I Analysed Them

The data are analysed under two thematic lenses. Firstly, they are reviewed under the social movement theories that inform their review under the technology theories, leading to a synthesis of the two. Each case is also examined individually and in tandem.

This sequential process is elaborated upon in the following chapters after the presentation of the theoretical approaches and conceptual tools. However, every step follows an iterative approach which attempts to include the participants' input in the whole undertaking. Jack Kloppenburg and others point out that the conceptual framing of alternative agriculture in academic research is primarily "based on the reflections of academics and policy specialists rather than on the views of sustainable producers" (2000, p.178), which, despite being valuable, may ignore the diverse empirically developed reflections of those involved in the movement. Similarly, within the wider discussion about the democratisation and assessment of technology development, the language of "participation" and "engagement" has been widely appropriated by political elites as an attempt to avoid criticism, while academic research has often focused on the introduction of novel institutional arrangements (like citizen forums) to tackle the issue than critically challenging the dichotomy between expert and lay participation (Thorpe 2008; Brown 2009; Levidow 2007).

The above indicates the limited empirically grounded research that adopts a bottom-up and inclusive framing of participatory technology development. This book is an attempt to bring forth the perspectives of those engaged in the development of technological artefacts for the agricultural production sector while being the ones working with these artefacts bridging knowledge, values and skill. To articulate their alternative conceptualisations of technology, the chapters presenting my empirical work heavily feature their voices rather than just mine. Additionally, analysis in the technology section (Chaps. 5 and 6) takes place in two levels. The ground level, which explores the interactions within the community, and a macro level, which evaluates the impact of socio-economic forces in both cases based on insight provided by critical theories of technology.

Chapters 3 and 5 establish the necessary framework, from a social movement and technology perspective, while Chaps. 4 and 6 provide the analysis respectively. In this sense, this current chapter does not offer a comprehensive description of how the data are analysed but rather a guide for how this research project is structured.

BIBLIOGRAPHY

Bauwens, M. (2005) "The Political Economy of Peer Production", *CTHEORY*, Available at: http://www.ctheory.net/articles.aspx?id=499, accessed 7 September 2008

Brown, M. (2009) *Science in Democracy: Expertise, Institutions and Representation*, Cambridge, MA: MIT Press

Kloppenburg, J., Lezberg, S., De Master, S., Stevenson, G. and Hendirckson, J. (2000) "Tasting Food, Tasting Sustainability: Defining the Attributes of an Alternative Food System with Competent Ordinary People", *Human Organisation*, 59(2), pp. 177–186

Levidow L. (2007) "European Public Participation as Risk Governance: Enhancing Democratic Accountability for Agbiotech Policy?", *East Asian Science, Technology and Society: An International Journal*, 1(1), pp. 19–51

Palys, T. and Atchison, C. (2008) *Research Decisions: Quantitative and Qualitative Perspectives*, Toronto: Thomson Nelson

Thorpe, C. (2008) "Political Theory in Science and Technology Studies", in Hackett, EJ, Amsterdamska, O, Lynch, M, Wajcman, J (eds) *The Handbook of Science and Technology Studies*, 3rd edition, Cambridge, MA: MIT Press, pp. 63–82

Yin, R.K. (2003) *Case Study Research: Design and Methods*, 3rd edition, Thousand Oaks: Sage

CHAPTER 3

Social Movements as Technology Developers

Abstract This chapter expands on the social movement theories that are utilised in this book. Specifically, resource mobilisation theory and framing analysis. These are presented and adapted in the context of the book to examine the material and immaterial considerations of the open source movement respectively. Meaning the impact resource availability and management have in the organisation and activity of social movement actors as well as the various cognitive processes that take place to justify and endorse action.

Keywords Resource mobilisation • Framing analysis • Master frames

Open source technology in agriculture is a phenomenon not easy to classify. As will I show in Chap. 4, while certain individuals within these communities do not classify themselves as the adherents of a specific social movement, they do see themselves as ideologically kindred to larger global movements that inform their activities even if some participate just because it makes practical sense. Open source agriculture is, therefore, a social movement emerging from the agglomeration of the various initiatives from around the world. Although, much like in the case of the free and open source movement, there are varying goals and backgrounds among

© The Author(s) 2019
C. Giotitsas, *Open Source Agriculture*, Palgrave Advances in
Bioeconomy: Economics and Policies,
https://doi.org/10.1007/978-3-030-29341-3_3

these initiatives, it is beneficial to determine whether there is collective action stemming from common political goals.

Social movements typically oppose an established status quo via protest or via promoting alternatives. In movements like the free and open source software one, a novel perspective of the term social movement was required because instead of contesting proprietary software, like typical oppositional movements would, it not only promoted an alternative, but it produced it. Hence, David Hess (2005) coined the term technology- and product-oriented movements to label those initiatives that create and promote specific technological artefacts and practices.

Technology- and product-oriented movements challenge scientific knowledge and certain technological systems. They promote or produce alternatives by establishing alliances with groups sharing similar interests like scientists and entrepreneurs (Hess et al. 2007). Examples of such movements can be found in various fields: the antismoking movement as oppositional to cancer; the HIV therapy movements as promoting alternatives in the health sector; the nuclear power and genetically modified food as oppositional movements to certain technologies; the organic food movement as promoting alternative agricultural methods in the environmental sector; the media reform oppositional movement and the open source, alternative media in the information sector.

I conceptualise the open source agriculture as such, and I assemble here the elements necessary to review open source agriculture under a similar vein.

3.1   SOCIAL MOVEMENT THEORIES

Social movement theory emerged in the beginning of the twentieth century. Early research was centred on the ideas of deprivation and grievances that pushed individuals to act spontaneously and often irrationally (see, e.g., the work of Gustave Le Bon and Neil Smelser). However, the proliferation of various social movements, with explicit goals, strategies and beliefs, required concrete theoretical frameworks and conceptual tools to be examined. The racial, women's and environmental movements are indicative examples.

The new theoretical approaches can be thematically divided into three streams. The first, influenced by organisation theory, examines predominantly social movement organisations at the core of social movements as hubs of strategic planning and coordination. The most prominent example of this stream is resource mobilisation theory (hereafter RM), introduced by McCarthy and Zald (1977). According to RM, social movements are not mere manifestations of grievances but expressions of rational collective action made possible by using available resources. To achieve this, social movements rely heavily upon organisations. These formal Social Movement Organisations (hereafter SMO) are examined in RM to establish how they mobilise a variety of resources and engage various actors to maintain the social movement and extend its influence.

The second stream borrows from political studies to examine social movements. Within this stream, political opportunity (or political process) theory focuses on the impact that institutions and political/structural factors might have on the success or failure of social movements (Tarrow 1998). According to this approach, political opportunities and changes in the political environments might have a profound impact on social movements, as they might enable or constrain collective action for certain social groups (McAdam 1998). Thus, the actions of social movements are viewed as reactions to changes in the political process.

The third stream views social movements through a cultural and social-constructivist lens. Sparked by new social movements, whose groups are formed on a shared identity like the LGBT or the women's movements, research here focuses on processes of construction of meaning and ideologies. Within this stream, framing analysis examines how social movements enable collective action through the construction of frames that provide a common identity and goals for the adherents (Snow and Benford 1988).

Social movement theories allow us to gauge the form of political structures within society, that is, the people's engagement in public issues (Tilly 2004). I selected framing and RM analysis because they provide conceptual tools to track the diverse set of values and interests represented in the cases as well as they examine the organisational forms of the SMOs under study and the selective incentives for individuals' participation. Political opportunity may not provide the right tools for insight in this case, since the political climate within which this movement is emerging is not shifting towards favourable conditions (an understatement according to many of those I conversed with). Elements of it however are implemented in the RM analysis; for instance, in exploring the securing of resources through state outlets and working around regulatory hindrances.

3.1.1   Framing Analysis

A frame is a methodological concept that describes the amalgam of ideas and perspectives that motivate individuals and groups (Goffman 1974). More specifically, the concept of collective action frames is used to describe "action-oriented sets of beliefs and meanings that inspire and legitimate the activities and campaigns of a social movement organization" (Benford and Snow 2000, p.614). These collective action frames are deployed "to mobilize potential adherents and constituents, to garner bystander support, and to demobilize antagonists" towards the achievement of the movements' goals (Snow and Benford 1988, p.198).

Some collective action frames may be so successful with applying these processes and acquire such a broad scope that they achieve a status of master frames. The master frames influence the activity and orientation of other movements. While regular collective action frames are specific and limited to the issue they attempt to address, master frames are wider and flexible allowing for various movements to use them. I consider master frames as symbolic tools with cultural significance in certain time periods, which allow various movements to adapt them in order to elicit support (Swart 1995). I explore how the open source agriculture movement is engaging in master frame alignment processes to reconfigure three master frames, namely the organic, open source and peasant ones to formulate its collective action frame.

Framing analysis systematically traces the various ideals, beliefs and ideologies that contribute into the emergence of open source technology as a social movement and subsequently a development model for alternative technology. It enables the exploration of the link between ideologies and action, which in this case goes beyond opposition to create artefacts imbued with these ideologies.

Frame alignment processes within each SMO are traced to identify the open source agriculture collective action frame. As a social construction, this frame is malleable and ever evolving, formulated in a transnational level by different types of actors engaging in productive activity rather than merely promoting a certain agenda. Framing analysis, then, helps understand how technology is produced in the context of the economic activity outside the dominant mode of technology production.

However, given that this mode of technology production partially relies on market and state relations, I assume that interests and values of these spheres also influence the technological outcome of the movement under study. This type of specialised social movement activity depends on material resources and the socio-economic environment it is taking place in. This is where resource mobilisation comes in, to provide further insight on what type of structure these organisations adopt to maintain their activity and what incentives are offered in their adherents to elicit support and resources.

3.1.2   Resource Mobilisation

Resource mobilisation (henceforth RM) emerged as a response to previous scholarship claiming that social movement activity is irrational and practiced by fringe members of society. Instead, RM maintains that social movements need resources to exist and act rationally to obtain them. The social movement here is viewed as a mobilised demand (or preference) for change in society (McCarthy and Zald 2001). The SMOs are important elements of representation for this demand, as they mobilise the necessary resources for the demand to be met.

There are three basic assumptions for RM: first, instead of being supported by aggrieved populations who provide resources, movements draw upon a wider base of supporters both individuals and groups; second, movements can use several tactics to achieve their goals; and third, movements interact with and are influenced by political and institutional structures, primarily through SMOs.

A SMO is defined as a formal organisation that aligns its interests with those of a social movement (ibid.). Several SMOs might be affiliated with one movement, grouped in a "social movement industry", and it is possible for them to be competing for the resources available for the achievement of the movement's goals (McCarthy and Zald 2003). These resources may include materials, money, labour, land, facilities, technical expertise or even legitimacy (Tilly 1978; McCarthy and Zald 1977).

For resources to be attained, the SMO focuses its actions towards the individuals and groups in society that may assist in the achievement of the movement's goals. These may be categorised in various ways. For the purpose of this book, I outline McCarthy and Zald's (1977) categorisation: generally speaking, there may be opponents to the movement's goals and mere bystanders; more importantly, those that share the movement's convictions are called adherents, while those that actively contribute resources to the achievement of the movement's goals are its constituents. A further distinction for each of these categories is whether they may benefit from the achievement of the groups goals or not as, presumably, even an opponent could potentially be a beneficiary. Having said that, an adherent or even a constituent is not necessarily a beneficiary as they might contribute out of simple agreement to the movement's cause.

In broad terms, the SMO attempts to turn bystanders into adherents (beneficiary or otherwise) and adherents into constituents, but the goal of each movement is what defines the specific course of action. A SMO may provide selective incentives that will ensure continuous involvement from constituents. These incentives may be monetary or material. Thus, RM examines social movements and SMOs to identify what groups and individuals are engaged and how resources are mobilised to achieve the movement's goals.

The focus of RM on SMOs and selective incentives, combined with the insights from motivation framing in the master frame analysis, allows for the examination of the organisational structures featured in both cases as well as the material motivation behind the involvement of individuals in the movement. RM enables their examination as rational actors pursuing goals that could be perceived as attempting to escape the prevailing socio-economic context of market relations in conventional agriculture, while struggling to secure the necessary resources to remain sustainable within it or at its periphery.

L'Atelier Paysan and Farm Hack are only two of the SMOs involved in the open source agriculture movement. They have been selected due to their extraordinary organisational structures and the large communities supporting them. The next chapter applies the theoretical approaches presented here in the two cases. First, L'Atelier Paysan and Farm Hack, as SMOs, are examined separately to pinpoint their unique characteristics as they are formulated within their respective environments even though they are geared towards similar goals.

Then, I review the three master frames identified as contributing in the open source agriculture collective action frame. Master frames here are considered historical thematic umbrellas to aggregate the immaterial underpinnings (values, ideals, interests, goals, etc.) of the movement. These have been identified via preliminary research in either case which included tentative interviews and a review of documents and online material. They were then synthesised through a mixture of extensive literature review on the topic of framings in the identified social movements as well as key documents of their prominent transnational SMOs. The frames are broad enough to encompass all relevant elements identified in the subcases.

No other broad frames were identified. I present each master frame, followed by its adaptation and application in either case. Last, I present an account of the overall case of the movement. All common elements are aggregated to formulate the collective action frame for the open source agriculture movement. It is the framework that offers a unified front encapsulating the diverse values and motivations as well as a common language for the whole movement. This forms the basis for the second part of analysis in this book, which borrows on theory of technology to apply the frame onto the technology development process emanating from within the movement.

BIBLIOGRAPHY

Benford, R.D. and Snow, D.A. (2000) "Framing Processes and Social Movements: An Overview and Assessment", *Annual Review of Sociology*, 26, pp. 611–639

Goffman, E. (1974) *Frame Analysis. An Essay on the Organization of Experience*, Boston: North-Eastern University Press

Hess, D. (2005) "Technology and Product Oriented Movements: Approximating Social Movement Studies and Science and Technology Studies", *Science, Technology & Human Values*, 30, pp. 513–535

Hess, D., Breyman, S., Campbell, N. and Martin, B. (2007) "Science, Technology, and Social Movements", in Hackett, E.J., Amstermdamska, O., Lynch, M. and Wacjman, J. (eds) *New Handbook of Science and Technology Studies*, Cambridge, MA: MIT Press

McAdam, D. (1998) "On the International Origins of Domestic Political Opportunities", in Costain, A.N. and McFarland, A.S. (eds) *Social Movements and American Political Institutions*, Lanham, MD: Rowman & Littlefield, pp. 251–267

McCarthy, J.D. and Zald, M. (1977) "Resource Mobilization and Social Movements: A Partial Theory", *American Journal of Sociology*, 82, pp. 1212–1241

McCarthy, J.D. and Zald, M. (2001) "The Enduring Vitality of the Resources Mobilisation Theory of Social Movements", in Turner, J. (ed) *Handbook of Sociological Theory*, New York: Kluwer Academic and Plenum Publishers

McCarthy, J.D. and Zald, M. (2003) "Social Movement Organizations", in Goodwin, J. and Jasper, J. (eds) *The Social Movement Reader: Cases and Concepts*, London: Blackwell

Snow, D.A. and Benford, R.D. (1988) "Ideology, Frame Resonance, and Participant Mobilization", *International Social Movement Research*, 1, pp. 197–217

Swart, W.J. (1995) "The League of Nations and the Irish Question: Master Frames, Cycles of Protest, and Master Frame Alignment", *The Sociological Quarterly*, 36, pp. 465–481

Tarrow, S. (1998) *Power in Movement: Social Movements, Collective Action, and Politics*, New York: Cambridge University Press

Tilly, T. (1978) *From Mobilization to Revolution*, Reading, MA: Addison-Wesley

Tilly, C. (2004) *Social Movements, 1768–2004*, Boulder, CO: Paradigm

CHAPTER 4

Open Source Agriculture: A Social Movement?

Abstract The two subcases of the book are examined here under the lens of social movement theory presented in the previous chapter. Each subcase is reviewed individually and then comparatively. Ultimately the chapter synthesises the open source agriculture movement's collective action frame. This frame is an amalgamation of characteristics found in three master frames identified in the movement. The open source frame, the organic frame and the peasant frame. These inform the nature and actions of the organisations active in the open source agriculture movement.

Keywords Farm Hack • L'Atelier Paysan • Collective action frame

4.1   THE SOCIAL MOVEMENT ORGANISATION OF L'ATELIER PAYSAN

L'Atelier Paysan literally translates as the peasant workshop. It emerged in 2009 as a subgroup within an association for the development and promotion of organic agriculture called ADAbio in Rhone-Alpes (a region in the south east of France). It all began when the founders of this project Joseph, an experienced organic farmer and a member of ADAbio, and Fabrice, a very politically aware carpenter and then agronomist, realised that farmers could genuinely benefit from each other's tool-building experience and creativity. So they standardised, documented and disseminated three essential pieces of machinery that had been developed by Joseph along with other farmers and were used in raised bed farming (one of the basic methods for soil management in organic agriculture).

This effort was well-received by the farmers in their network so more tool-building knowledge was accumulated over the next three years from farms in the area. Sixteen farmer-built tools were standardised in total. Their designs were then printed in a comprehensive guide-book complete with blueprints and pictures, for more farmers to be able to construct them in their own farm. Prints of the book were sold to support their activities while its digital version is available on the website for anyone to access (along with an invitation for users to translate it into other languages).

Meanwhile, in 2011 the first workshop took place. The tools made by L'Atelier Paysan are, almost, entirely made of metal. Ten farmers attended the workshop to learn how to work metal (basically cut, drill and weld) and attempt to assemble some of the aforementioned tools. The workshop was quite successful with the farmers producing eight tools by the end of a week. At this point, these farmers along with Joseph and Fabrice established ADAbio Autoconstruction, which was basically the branch of ADAbio that was promoting the self-building of machinery by farmers.

To facilitate the demand for more activity, first using various internship programmes funded by the French state and later through regional state funds, they managed to hire people with specific sets of skills to assist in their endeavour, like for instance engineers and political economy graduates. After that, the first season of workshops began, where farmers learned metal-work and built the first three machines. Initially, this activity was exclusive to their local region but later expanded in others.

While their workshops started attracting more farmers from all over France, the group began developing more tools along with farmers not limited to organic market gardening but included all types of small-scale farming. For instance, they work with wine and fruit producers, cattle farmers and farmers using horse power. As their activity expanded, ADAbio could no longer facilitate this work, so in 2014 L'Atelier Paysan was founded. As a legal entity, L'Atelier Paysan is a cooperative whose stakeholders are the individual constituents (mainly farmers) and groups (other farming and solidarity organisations) that belong in the wider network of L'Atelier Paysan. Its base of operations is in the Rhone-Alpes region while one of the first engineers to have worked in the project has established a branch in the region of Brittany (north-west).

4.1.1 Organisational Structure

L'Atelier Paysan was initially conceived by a group of farmers led by Joseph and Fabrice. Their activity was institutionalised through ADAbio, the organic farming association they were all part of, forming ADAbio Autoconstruction. Within ADAbio, they managed to secure initially funds for paid internships and later regional funding to employ an engineer and a development officer. This enabled them to expand their activity and the number of farmers involved. Over the years, it became apparent that ADAbio could no longer facilitate this operation.

As my key informant Julien, a political science graduate with a focus on social economy, puts it, "We were an association so each farmer trained by us needed to be part of it. We had a core team of farmers elected by the members of the association. This core team did a lot of everyday decision making and ultimately it was not the right way to invest their energy available for this project". So the decision was made to create the not-for-profit cooperative that was named L'Atelier Paysan, and now the core group engages in strategic planning and general direction while the operational team can make everyday decisions without the explicit consent of the cooperative. The structure of the organisation could be illustrated as an inverted pyramid with the cooperative at the top, the core group in the middle and the operational team in charge of implementing the action plans and day to day decision-making at the bottom.

The constituents, directly involved in the endeavour, were invited to become shareholders in the cooperative to contribute to the decision-making process. They basically form the L'Atelier Paysan network, which includes various active farmers, farming associations, solidarity associations, groups that assist farmers and individuals that are active contributors to the mission of L'Atelier Paysan. Shareholders meet physically at least once per year in their general assembly. Their annual meeting involves discussing what has been achieved the previous year, plans for the next year, voting for the admission of new shareholders and various activities and promotional events.

Furthermore, the core group of L'Atelier Paysan convenes over the telephone, as the constituents are spread all over France, once per month to discuss current issues. This group is comprised of shareholders, but often enough, other people with a special skillset or insight on various current issues are invited to participate. These people may ultimately end up joining the shareholder group if their contribution is considered valuable.

For instance, a farmer with previous experience as a patent lawyer was invited in 2015 to provide counsel for a potential infringement case. He later became a shareholder as well. Similarly, a farmer/web developer working on the L'Atelier Paysan website also became a shareholder.

The cooperative has several full-time employees as well as volunteers (paid) tasked with the various essential activities. While many do not have a background in agriculture, it was made obvious through the interviews conducted with them that they all share the vision of L'Atelier Paysan. Besides Joseph and Fabrice, who act as CEOs of the cooperative, there are a number of engineers, architects, a web developer and other individuals in charge of administration, development and dissemination. Several of these employees (as well as previous ones) have become shareholders in the cooperative over the years.

The size of the operational group of the cooperative is considered ideal, given the available resources, to facilitate the amount of activities decided upon by the cooperative. Should the need for further expansion come up, the group is reluctant to increase the size and complexity of its activities which would in turn reduce their capacity for direct communication and cooperation with farmers. Instead they propose the creation of more groups similar to theirs which would form a network of cooperation and solidarity.

4.1.2   Economic Model

L'Atelier Paysan has developed a unique model to secure monetary resources for its activity, tailored to the French socio-economic context. In Julien's words: "We come from the world of associations so we know it is difficult to run a healthy business model with an association because it relies heavily on subsidies. This is not really massive right now, state funds I mean". They needed more autonomy and a way to produce some profit to help the whole project develop, hence their elaborate model to acquire resources.

The L'Atelier Paysan cooperative is non-profit. Its shareholders receive no dividends and the shares are not re-invested. Whatever positive balance the cooperative has every year goes into an indivisible reserve that funds their activities. Acquiring a share will provide the shareholder with the capacity to influence the decision-making of the L'Atelier Paysan network but not much else. By redeeming it, the shareholder will either receive the original value invested or less if losses have occurred. L'Atelier Paysan does not sell its services to individuals or other companies. Instead, to secure funds for its operations, L'Atelier Paysan has developed a multifaceted support model.

Initially, it relied mostly on the contributions of the founding farmers and some regional funds for rural development. Over time the workshops became established providing important financial resources for the organisation. Contributions by farmers participating in the workshops make up for a large percentage of the budget. These resources are allocated towards the development of new technology, the maintenance of L'Atelier Paysan's equipment and the dissemination of the work, as well as support the participation of farmers who are unable to contribute.

However, by tapping into a special mutualised state fund (in collaboration with a public-interest organisation which is eligible for income tax relief) for vocational training and skill development, L'Atelier Paysan manages to secure reimbursements for most or all of the contribution each farmer makes. Furthermore, they buy raw material and equipment in bulk and then resell them to farmers at below market prices yet still making a very small profit. Nevertheless, they do not manufacture nor sell any of the machines that they produce, besides those produced in the workshops which are then acquired by the farmers that pay for the materials.

Further, financial support comes from crowdfunding as well as various solidarity organisations. For instance, associations for solidarity financing groups from all over France offer their support to L'Atelier Paysan. Last, important financial support comes from national and regional funds for agriculture that have recognised L'Atelier Paysan's contribution to the development of agriculture in France. Though the group feels that it would be best to reduce the percentage of this type of support for reasons that will be further explored later in the book. All the financial activity is made public in the L'Atelier Paysan website to ensure transparency.

4.1.3   Operational Capacity

The operational activity of L'Atelier Paysan is two-fold: on the one hand, they engage in research and development of new technology, and on the other, they disseminate technological know-how. These may be considered the main social movement activities L'Atelier Paysan devotes resources to. Resources are allocated in more traditional SMO activities, like organising an annual gathering/festival for dissemination workshops and other activities as well as producing promotional material (like leaflets, posters, even books). Yet the focus is on the productive capacity of the SMO rather than relying solely on advocacy, absorbing the bulk of their available resources. Providing the farmers with practical solutions is deemed a more effective way to communicate their ideological convictions and achieve the movement's missions.

4.1.3.1 Knowledge Transfer

The first of the two main goals of L'Atelier Paysan is enabling farmers to create their own machines and tools. L'Atelier Paysan is based in the region of Rhone-Alpes along with its branch in Brittany. However, they own three fully equipped trucks that function as mobile workstations that help them to transfer their activity all over France. They conduct workshops that last three to five days in farms, warehouses or any other space that could facilitate them. The nature, location and time of the workshops are defined by the farmers themselves at the end of each year according to their specific needs and time availability.

The farmers attending might have some previous experience but often they do not. They usually tend to be engaging in similar agricultural activity, so the machines built in each workshop target a certain need of the specific group. The farmers that provide the funds for the materials get to keep the machine(s) at the end of the workshop.

4.1.3.2 Technology Development and Dissemination

L'Atelier Paysan started as an attempt to gather, systematise and disseminate essential farm equipment created by farmers. This is still a primary goal for L'Atelier Paysan. For this reason, its people travel across the country, meeting with farmers and gathering information on farming equipment and later farm buildings as well. This information is codified and uploaded to the L'Atelier Paysan forum for anyone to access.

Several groups and individual farmers have been inspired by L'Atelier Paysan and have created machines that were later uploaded in the forum. The forum post includes the design and pictures of the various versions of the machine. There are over 500 posts in the forum containing instructions and conversations regarding farm machines, methods and buildings.

Beyond that, L'Atelier Paysan enables the creation of new technology from farmers. Machines that are either non-existent on the marketplace, too expensive or not suitable for small-scale and organic farming. These machines need to be modular, easy to replicate using materials that can be upcycled or easily sourced. However, in order for L'Atelier Paysan to engage in a project, the ethical principles of the community must be met. A group of at least five farmers with a specific need or idea needs to be formed, since L'Atelier Paysan does not work with individuals. Then an engineer-facilitator is assigned to the project and the design process begins. After several meetings and feedback exchanges, a design is finalised and the prototyping process begins.

This process may also take place to improve or modify an already existing machine. Further, L'Atelier Paysan may work with other groups, beyond farmers, that produce tools for farming provided they share the same principles. For instance, the "Aggrozouk", a pedal-powered tractor, was developed by an independent group of makers called Farming Soul. L'Atelier Paysan was later invited to help improve the machine. All these processes are further explored in Chap. 6 that focuses on technology development.

4.1.4 Selective Incentives for Participation

The farmers participating in these activities may be considered constituents of L'Atelier Paysan after having adopted an active role. They potentially were adherents to the L'Atelier Paysan cause before or just bystanders that were exposed to the activity. At any rate, the incentives for joining the cause are multiple and evident. After all, the point of the organisation is to help their constituents while attempting to politically engage them in their cause. As Julien points out, the goal was "to create an organisation that would be a hub of resources, of farmers exchanging knowledge and know-how with the support of a team of workers. This would make the process faster than remaining farm-based which would be limited", while also being "a good start for them to rethink their practices and have the right tools to change them".

Therefore, regarding material incentives, these farmers gain valuable skills, in most cases without any significant cost due to the aforementioned vocational training fund. This enables them to support their agricultural activity more efficiently by making their own tools and machinery as well as maintain their already existing equipment. Furthermore, they gain access to materials and manufacturing equipment that they use, with the help of L'Atelier Paysan, to build machinery tailored to their needs with relatively little cost. This enables them to tap into the productive capacities of their peers that also participate, enabling them to form partnerships.

For instance, a group of goat farmers, along with L'Atelier Paysan, created a rather large seeding machine (the prototyping workshop of which I attended) that they would collaboratively use in their fields, instead of having to invest to acquire one each.

As far as immaterial resources are concerned, the general knowledge exchange, the sense of community and working together appear to be strong incentives as was indicated to me by a farmer. He points out that while in the past the term paysan (person that lives in the land) was mostly used to describe farmers, in recent years it has been widely replaced by "exploitant argicole" (roughly translated as exploiter of the land), which according to him indicates the current status of commodification in agriculture. The practical application of L'Atelier Paysan's alternative methods and processes is considered the most convincing argument one can make to promote the movement's goals.

4.1.5   The Social Movement Organisation of Farm Hack

Farm Hack emerged as a collaborative effort of farmer activists. It was conceived as a gathering to brainstorm ideas for various tool-related problems in a farm. This first Farm Hack event was a big success, leading to the hosting of several more events in the USA and later all over the world. It also led to the establishment of a large and decentralised community comprised mostly of farmers. From within the Farm Hack community emerged a digital platform that functions as communication, coordination, dissemination and, to some degree, technology development tool. Primarily the platform functions as a database of tools that have been built, modified and shared by the community. The tools are released under a Creative Commons license for everyone to use and modify freely, provided they will release the designs under a similarly open licence.

Farm Hack was established in 2011 after the first event organised by members of the Greenhorns and the National Young Farmers Coalition, non-profits that provide support for young and small-scale farmers in the USA, in collaboration with engineers from the Massachusetts Institute of Technology (MIT). Farm Hack inspired by the open source culture would bring together farmers, designers, engineers, academics and activists in events to engage in dialogue; skill development; tool design, building and demonstration. The results were then documented in the Farm Hack platform for other farmers to access them. Over time the platform was joined and enriched by farmers from all over the USA but also other countries and to this date features more than 500 tools. The content can be accessed by everyone and is open to improve or modify to whomever joins the platform (along with the platform itself).

4.1.6 Organisational Structure

Farm Hack had no legal entity of its own at the time of its conception nor any type of dedicated organisation. Instead, resources were provided by the non-profits, which primarily organised the Farm Hack events and built the platform. It relied on volunteer work from the expanding Farm Hack community to build the platform and run the events. In the early years of the community, the activity was centralised and guided by the participating organisations, specifically the Greenhorns and the National Young Farmers Coalition.

Farm Hack acquired a non-profit status in 2013, when the community grew. Having a legal form, it managed to receive some funding through grants to improve platform and provide resources for the short-term employment of two of its constituents, who worked on community outreach. After this point, the community became more independent and decentralised. It now relies entirely on the support and time of its constituents as well as its partnerships with other organisations rather than attempt to secure its own resources to employ personnel. This has, inevitably, led to reduced momentum, given that everyone is contributing in their free time. Yet the consensus in the community is that it should keep relying on the constituents' voluntary contribution rather than employ workers for its operations, remaining independent and faithful to their principles. This structure allows them to operate in a relatively low risk, low maintenance and distributed mode.

Farm Hack lacks formal structure. As a non-profit, it has a board of directors; however, its role is mostly nominal. Instead, every member of the community is free to contribute to the decision-making process. Practically, this means that the constituents most engaged in Farm Hack end up being the ones most involved in the organisational structure. A do-ocracy of sorts as one of the interviewees with a software development background and a key developer of the Farm Hack platform, puts it. Weekly coordination virtual meetings would take place as well, which are open to whomever desired to participate. The platform has been incrementally improved over the years to provide an easier and more independent service to the users and reduce the effort required for its expansion and upkeep. Thus making, for instance, the tool documentation process better as well as providing a detailed template for users and affiliated organisations/groups to organise Farm Hack events autonomously.

4.1.7   Economic Model

Farm Hack, as a non-profit organisation and a community, does not engage in any type of commercial activity. For its operations, it relies mostly on the contributions of its constituents and initially on the resources of the participating organisations. After acquiring the non-profit status, its collaborations with other groups allow it to use their resources as well. There have been instances where some small grants have been acquired in collaboration with other organisations. These funds were directed towards employing community constituents, who were already volunteering their work to Farm Hack. They would work more intensely for short periods of time, namely on improving and maintaining the platform and community coordination. A topic under discussion within the community is whether acquiring funds to employ individuals for more systematic documentation of tools should be pursued.

Some of the most active farmer-inventors contributing tools in the platform have invested a considerable amount of their time and resources in prototyping and documenting. Another important topic within the community is how to enable a business ecosystem to thrive around the platform that may provide sustainability to individuals and groups dedicated to the Farm Hack principles. Individuals are free to engage in commercial activities. As long as the basic principle is maintained, that of openly sharing, users may add in the description of their contributed tools that they can also sell them or some sort of service to those that would prefer to purchase rather than invest the time and effort to create a tool themselves.

The Farm Hack platform features a commerce component where "businesses and organizations invite other users in to see what they have been working on, the events they have hosted or will host, the tools they've worked on, and the conversations they've been involved with". Their goal with this open shop initiative is to provide a simplified toolset for users or groups to sell their tools or parts or even certain services as well as spaces with fabrication or educational capacity. Commerce is considered important according to the Farm Hack ethos as "regionalized manufacturing makes for resilient economies and tools which are customized to a farmer's particular needs".

4.1.8   Operational Capacity

The operations of Farm Hack revolve around activity in the platform and the events, with documentation from those events resulting in the platform. During the early years, the Farm Hack events were mostly organised and facilitated by the organisations that invested their own resources on Farm Hack activities. Over time, as the community grew more independent and decentralised, a detailed guide for events was developed and featured in the platform to enable the constituents and affiliated organisations to host events as an attempt to distribute the resource requirements across the Farm Hack network.

In general, these events are problem-solving oriented with various specific goals. For instance, they may involve conceptual meetings to brainstorm new tools; collaboratively design, build or document tools; skill and know-how transfer; and software hackathons. Documentation of results, regardless of the focus of each event, is always encouraged in order for the entire community to benefit from these events. Further, these events are opportunities to attract new adherents and constituents (as well as for existing ones to socialise).

The Farm Hack platform is the second point of operational activity. It has been developed by community constituents with software development skills, and it is based on various other open source tools. The platform serves both as a coordination and collaboration tool for the community and as tool database for the ones that have been individually or collective produced. While there has been a steady influx of users and tools, the platform has not been very successful as a collaboration tool, with most of the coordination happening "behind the scenes" and the collaborative tool design taking place in physical spaces, like the events, rather than digital. Further, proper documentation of both processes and tools is an issue that the core group is trying to improve, as it is a resource heavy process.

4.1.9   Selective Incentives for Participation

Similarly to the L'Atelier Paysan case, several incentives are available here for potential constituents. The Farm Hack platform features hundreds of tools that farmers can adapt to their needs. Moreover, the events present opportunities for valuable knowledge exchange and collaboration. Unlike the L'Atelier Paysan case however, financial resources are much more limited in Farm Hack. Relying almost entirely on individual resource contribution, Farm Hack has enabled commercial activity to be developed around the platform with the hope that constituents/entrepreneurs/tool developers would support the Farm Hack activity while making a sustainable living within the community.

Interviewee A and Tim, two of the farmer/engineers from Farm Hack, exemplify this. Combining engineering and agricultural knowledge, they invest considerable resources in the development of new tools in collaboration with farmers of the Farm Hack community. To maintain their activity, they experiment with various methods to secure resources. These include crowdfunding campaigns, organising workshops similar to the L'Atelier Paysan ones, offering manufacturing services to other farmers, bidding for (the admittedly limited) support grants for agriculture, selling the tools themselves or partly assembled kits. This is an aspect of Farm Hack still under development, and a best course of action has not been determined yet. The difficulties are evident for these individual entrepreneurs, and making their activity in the community sustainable is a constant struggle. However, they recognise that engaging in this activity within the community is preferable to doing so outside it. As interviewee A notes, "It would be a hard business plan for me to take the development costs up to myself for every tool I build. But if there's an ocean of designs on Farm Hack and people come to me to build someone else's design then the one tool I develop and contribute the design for can be amortized over all the other tools I'm building". Further, the platform enables the capacity for feedback to further improve on their tools.

Another, farmer/inventor, interviewee having distanced himself from the community after feeling frustrated by the community's inability to provide enough support for the prototyping of new tools, attempts to continue his activity independently in his own business. He finds though that this too proves quite difficult to achieve without a community to draw support/clients from. He says he would consider engaging with the Farm Hack community again. The open shops feature is a step towards enabling entrepreneurial activity in line with the community's principles. Yet ultimately the community itself will determine how this aspect of Farm Hack is going to evolve, if at all.

4.1.10   Resource Mobilisation in the Movement

Typically SMOs tend to compete for the finite resources within a social movement which in turn influences the tactics adopted to achieve their goals (Soule and King 2008). In this case however, given this movement's transnational scope, competition, at least between these two cases, does not appear to be a factor. On the contrary, there is collaboration, where possible, with members of either community calling the other "cousins". Cousins because they realise that there are considerable differences amongst them stemming from socio-political as well as cultural differences between France and the USA.

For instance, the fact that the French receive considerable resources from the state allows them to be more active and organised than their American peers. Financial resources mean that L'Atelier Paysan can employ constituents to work full-time in its various activities leading to some degree of professionalisation within the SMO. This professionalisation inadvertently creates a more centralised structure of operations. Consequently, it enables L'Atelier Paysan to provide a lot of support to farmers and have a very productive and standardised output (i.e., machines and tools), but could potentially hinder independent initiative within the community, as evidenced by the low degree of user tool submissions in L'Atelier Paysan forum.

On the other hand, lack of resources for Farm Hack means that the community depends heavily on independent initiative to achieve its goals, hence the desire to provide enough selective incentives, namely the capacity for commercial activity, to elicit participation. This is further enhanced by the lack of mistrust towards market relations in the USA context and the potential impact these might have on Farm Hack's activity, which according to Fabrice is more prominent in France and specifically L'Atelier Paysan community. As a result, Farm Hack's structure is loose and decentralised to be maintained even in periods of high inactivity. Its output is more diverse that way, but less standardised and not as well documented as L'Atelier Paysan.

Despite their differences, the target group of either SMO as well as their broad goals are similar, if not the same. Also, both cases share the conviction that the best approach to achieve their long-term goals is by providing tangible results instead of advocating change like most social movements. Eliciting participation in Farm Hack comes from "cascading networks to find people who would be excited to join us", Dorn, a farmer inventor and leading figure in Farm Hack, points out. Severine, a founding member and farming community organiser, also mentions that the various movements Farm Hack taps into are well networked and offer much dissemination to their work. Similarly in L'Atelier Paysan, the extensive network of farming associations allows the recruitment of farmers that are both partial to the agricultural model L'Atelier Paysan promotes but also conventional ones with the hopes of convincing them to convert.

Each case has developed a unique model to achieve this. Yet the narrative of both shares a strong focus on the utility of tools developed within their activity as a powerful argument to garner the attention of constituents looking to elevate the quality of their work and tackle everyday problems through their engagement in the movement. Furthermore, resource exchange between the two happens on the level of design and know-how, with several instances of knowledge sharing for the development of identical or similar tools. This is especially important considering how "closed off are the information pathways in agriculture across borders" as Kristen, another farmer and active member of the Farm Hack community, says. For instance, the Aggrozouk that was mentioned earlier in the L'Atelier Paysan case was initially inspired by the Culticycle that is developed within Farm Hack. This aspect is key and is discussed in the last two chapters. Next, I attempt to identify the ideological and cultural factors in each case that play into the formulation of a collective action frame for the movement.

4.2   FRAMING THE OPEN SOURCE AGRICULTURE MOVEMENT

Preliminary analysis has indicated three master frames prevalent in the framing of the movement, namely the open source, the organic and the peasant frames. Master frames in the sense that they are not specific to one movement but influence and orient the activities of several, often similar, movements due to their flexibility and capacity for cultural resonance (Benford and Snow 2000).

Identifying them was a relatively straightforward task. Clear references were elicited in texts, early interviews (with people outright mentioning them) and media in either case. Further, the type of farming activity the farmers engage in is also an indicator, meaning most are small-scale, independent and organic farmers. Other, more specialised collective action frames can also be identified, but their influence has been aggregated under these three master frames.

A bibliographical synthesis of each master frame follows as well as a detailed description of how these frames are adapted in each case. Then, I aggregate it to provide the collective action frame for the movement.

4.2.1   The Open Source Master Frame

The open source frame encompasses the activity of various social movements that share the principle of "openness". This section explores its development.

The open source master frame traces its roots in the late 1970s with the free software and its primary proponent, Richard Stallman. As a computer programmer at the MIT, he worked alongside other programmers/hackers under a regime of sharing the code in order to collaboratively develop it (Stallman 2002). However, this environment of openness eroded over the years, with various enclosures creeping in to limit the access to the code. In 1982, he began developing his own collection of free applications, GNU (Gnu is Not Unix) which would emulate the functions of the Unix system. In 1984, Stallman quit his job and devoted his efforts to the establishment of the Free Software Foundation (FSF), an SMO dedicated to the promotion of free software through the use of the GNU General Public License (GPL), a "copyleft" (an inversion of the term copyright) license that enables the creation and free distribution of code, as well as ensures that the code will remain free. Free as in free speech and not free beer as the free software advocates like to put it.

Next, I present three distinct but also intertwining social movements. These are the free software movement and the open source software movement (often presented and researched as one under the acronym FOSS), the open hardware movement and the open source appropriate technology movement. All three share the broad principles of the open source master frame, which can be summarised as (1) collaborative and decentralised development of artefacts that may be software, tools, machines, food, medicine and even houses; (2) the release of these artefacts under licenses that allow free access and redistribution over the internet; (3) a distinct governance model inspired by the open source development model that relies on transparency, open and autonomous participation, and flexible and meritocratic hierarchies.

4.2.1.1   The Free and Open Source Software Movement

The free software movement framed its activity through four freedoms that represent the ethos of its proponents. These freedoms were deemed essential for the building of community and consistently represent the values and ethics of the movement and are presented as "the right thing to do". Elliott and Scacchi (2008) distinguish three transformative periods in the free software movement's frame, calling this period the freedom frame.

In 1991, Linus Torvalds along with collaborating volunteers over the internet released a free version of the operating system UNIX, called Linux, which used the components of GNU. Linux was developed with the assistance of an online community and quickly it became as reliable as other marketable version of UNIX. The development model of Linux, which was based on a new version released weekly according to feedback by the user community, was quite radical, and over the years its efficiency was widely recognised.

As interest in Linux increased and businesses distributing it emerged, several key software developers, with the support of Torvalds and activist developer Raymond (1998), adopted the term open source software instead of free. The justification for this transformation on the frame was two-fold: first, the term free caused confusion as to what free really means, and second that it would be more pragmatic and friendlier to businesses who would be willing to support the mainstreaming of free software (Raymond 1997). A second SMO, called the Open Source Initiative (OSI), was established along with a set of principles outlining the trans-formed frame. The "business frame" as Elliott and Scacchi (2008) call it. Its principles relied mostly on pragmatism that focuses on the advantages of the open source development model, like for instance its reliability and low cost, rather than the ethics and freedom of the previous period. New licenses were established to facilitate these principles that embraced the marketing of open source software in the business world but ensured the openness. In other words, these licences provide more liberties, with regards to commercialisation, than the GPL (for instance, they allow the combination of proprietary and free software).

The success of the open source development model has brought about another transformation in the frame, which Elliott and Scacchi (2008) call the "occupational frame". The emergence of a business ecosystem around open source software, which also incorporates the open source principles in their structures, has expanded the capacity for employment within software communities, amplifying with it the growth of the open source frame beyond its original limited communities of enthusiasts.

The differences between FSF and the OSI created tensions that remain to this day. Yet the fact is that most pieces of open source software are also, in essence, free software and are treated as one and the same by many. In this vein, the open source software frame is viewed as an extension of the free software as it encompasses its goals and draws support from the same pool of adherents and constituents.

4.2.1.2 The Open Source Hardware Movement
The open source software movement can be considered a predecessor for the open source hardware movement that became prominent in the first decade of the twenty-first century. This movement appropriates the open source frame but may trace its roots to the hacker community that emerged in the late 1960s. Initially active in the intersection between software and computer hardware, this movement sought to apply the open source principles into hardware.

Several initiatives appeared that aimed to do so in the late 1990s. Perens (1997) launched the Open Hardware certification programme for devices whose programme interface would be open. Similar attempts to frame open hardware followed after, but most disappeared due to inactivity. Nevertheless, over the years, various open source hardware projects appeared like the RepRap 3D printer and the Arduino microcontroller. These projects developed large communities around them, and the open source hardware movement was revitalised. Initially, the open source software licenses were used to protect their openness, but over time several organisations appeared along with dedicated open hardware licenses. The CERN (European Organization for Nuclear Research) for instance created its own open hardware license in 2011 "in the spirit of knowledge and sharing and dissemination" (CERN 2017).

After much debate within the community and the various initiatives the Open Source Hardware Definition was formulated, which is based on the definition of the open source software. The definition frames the movement's activity under a set of principles which highlight unrestricted access, sharing of all relevant information and ease of modification. These principles are more in line with the framing of the open source rather than the free software. Further, the open source hardware association was formed, an SMO that would promote the movement's goals and standards, study the movement and disseminate its work, and provide guidance according to the movement's values and principles.

The open source hardware movement's frame has encompassed the maker and do-it-yourself communities discourse as well (Hatch 2014), while a growing number of open hardware projects greatly boosted by the proliferation of digital fabrication tools (like 3D printers and CNC machines) and the various spaces that enable making like fablabs, hackerspaces, makerspaces and so on have contributed into its wider dissemination (for more on these spaces, see Smith et al. 2013; Kostakis et al. 2014; Niaros et al. 2017). Similarly, action in these communities is framed around empowering individuals and communities to experiment, create locally and share globally artefacts or services to address their needs (Nascimento and Pólvora 2016).

4.2.1.3 The Open Source Appropriate Technology movement

The appropriate technology (also termed intermediate technology) movement's roots go back into the 1960s and was later popularised by the influential work of economist Ernst Friedrich Schumacher *Small Is Beautiful* (1973). Appropriate technology was initially conceived against the importing of western industrial level technology in developing countries, which were not suitable for the local socio-economic conditions. Hence, they ended up being either idle infrastructure or even detrimental to local communities. This technology would be located somewhere in the middle of traditional, labour-intensive technology and capital-intensive, industrialised technology.

While there are various definitions in the literature, the movement framed its activity around the development of technology that can be summarised as of low cost; locally and collaboratively designed and produced using local materials; small in scale and complexity yet suitable for groups of people and mindful of environmental and social concerns (Willoughby 1990; Hazeltine and Bull 1999).

For two decades, until the mid-1980s, several SMOs, state and private, were established in both developed and developing countries to promote the movement's goals. Yet by the end of the decade, activity was significantly reduced and most SMOs seized to exist. The reasons were multiple. First, the movement emerged in a period of disillusionment with the industrialisation programmes of the 1950s and 1960s which resulted in a lot of support in the form of resources that over time were severely diminished as neoliberal policies and market-based development were established (Morrison 1983). Second, there was not enough opposition against those benefiting from the incumbent technological systems, like large construction and manufacturing companies, agribusiness, large private utilities (Pursell 1993). Third, the very definition of the appropriate technology was so broad that it created inconsistencies and technical difficulties in its applications as well as too much external engagement with little involvement of the people for whom this technology was supposed to be for (Zelenika and Pearce 2011).

However, in 2000s, the appropriate technology movement frame has been transformed due to the proliferation of ICT and the emergence of the open source movement. The open sharing of designs using open source licences and the collaborative development are brought to the front in the open source appropriate movement. The framing of the movement is extended to include the efficiency of the free and open source software development model into appropriate tools and machinery; its acceleration of innovation due to easy and patent-free access to information; as well as access to technology that has been developed elsewhere and is accessible over the internet (Pearce and Mushtaq 2009). SMOs that develop appropriate technology have embraced the open source model and are sharing knowledge openly.

4.2.1.4 *The Open Source Master Frame in L'Atelier Paysan*

L'Atelier Paysan appropriated the open source frame soon after becoming active. They have engaged with the open source movement and adopted a Creative Commons license (typically used for openly sharing music, photographs, films, etc.) to make the design files of the machines available. They have been vocal about the merits of collaborative designing and manufacturing machines and then sharing their effort with other farmers. Pointing out the collaborative nature of the tool development procedure rather than just focusing on the open availability, the machine design files indicate a strong influence from the open source frame and the open source development processes it promotes. As the L'Atelier Paysan platform states: "We would like to create an open source Encyclopedia, where people can freely contribute and make use of resources available. We believe that farming skills are common goods, which should be freely disseminated and adapted".

The farmers I interacted with during my field work in the various L'Atelier Paysan events approved of the open source approach with a few noting that a strong reason for their attendance was the joy of sharing and producing something together. A topic of discussions during the cooperative's general assembly (and open annual gathering of L'Atelier Paysan) was the use of open source software like design software for the tool blueprints. The operational team of L'Atelier Paysan explained that while they would prefer free and open source software, the proprietary one (Solidworks) they use allows them to illustrate the design in a much more comprehensive way. No open source alternative can do that currently. It was decided to, at least, export the designs in open source formats rather than the proprietary one of Solidworks. Another discussion, about patents, had the largest attendance in the gathering. All attendees felt strongly against them with the consensus being that while patents were originally introduced to protect the livelihood of creators, nowadays it is an issue of profit making for big companies.

In the interviews conducted with the members of the cooperative, use of the open source vocabulary is also evident. Joseph, a prolific inventor farmer and the soul of the whole initiative, says, "My capacity (to build tools) comes from other people, family; friends; farmers I met from traveling around the world, it is only natural to give it back". With regards to open source licences, he adds, "The machines we built all those years ago are a lot better today because people have adapted and modified them. That would not be possible with patents. It is just logic; natural". The feeling is mutual for Gregoire, one of the engineers in the group. He says, "Open source seems logical to me, to share without barriers", and adds, "when the prototype is ready we need to protect the idea fast, so we make it available with the creative commons license and we specify that this is a prototype at the moment and we don't know if it is ok for every use". Meaning to ensure its openness from potential third parties that would appropriate and patent on it.

Fabrice, the second founder of the initiative, shares this view. He says, "All my career has been about giving somebody else the information that I have" which is why he created a couple of publication about ecology. He continues, "I didn't have any political conviction about open source hardware. But then I became specialised in organic agronomy, and I met hundreds of farmers. I saw that many were adapting and creating their tools like Joseph". After this creative friction and their first attempts to assist farmers, they initiated their "political project about autonomy and open source in agriculture". With regards to the movement in agriculture, he believes that the movement about open source seeds is strong, but not tools. He says, "Tools influence the lives of farmers. The agronomy—how they organise their day. So tools are important, as important as seeds".

He continues, "Our goal was to insert ourselves in bigger movements" including the open source and commons movements. This is how they were exposed to other open source tool initiatives like Farm Hack and Open Source Ecology (an initiative that has received wider media coverage). Although he quickly notes regarding the latter that "it is not the same experience because users are not included in the creative process. It's a top to bottom approach. It is a big concept, like a teaser for a movie but users are not involved". An opinion shared amongst some of the Farm Hack people I talked to as well (this was partly the reason why this particular project was not selected as a case for this book, despite its very ambitious and relevant scope).

Julien, while describing the development process, says that keywords like "collaborative, participatory, user innovation, open source" often appear. He says that these terms are fashionable, so their use could help them secure state funding in the uncertain future of the newly elected right-wing government. Further, the tools that end up in the platform are the "appropriate" ones to satisfy "collective needs", and besides that they also openly publish the various photographs, videos, documents and notes on the forum in order to spark "inspiration". All in accordance with the open source frame.

Though while he thinks it is good if people are inspired by their work, he is a bit sceptical of many of the actors in the wider open source movement, echoing Fabrice's sentiment. As Julien words it, "We would like to tell them that there are other ways to promote open source and develop technology. Their promotion and their methodology for development is often demagogique (grandstanding). They are so desperate to find real applications for the, very good, idea of open source that they endorse any project without filtering. That is not a good methodology and is doing a disservice to the movement". Meaning that a lot of these projects are not collectively developed and often do not correspond to real needs. He attributes this to entrepreneurship with the drive of the start-up culture, which is blooming within the open source movement, to create something new whether it is for the social good or not.

L'Atelier Paysan has appropriated the more radical "free" elements of the open source frame rather than simply treating it as an alternative development model. Focus is placed on the collaborative way of designing and producing tools that ultimately tackle the real needs of farmers. It is also placed on the critique of the patent system that is viewed as outdated, preventing farmers from accessing affordable and appropriate tools and enabling big companies to control how agricultural production is evolving.

4.2.1.5 The Open Source Master Frame in Farm Hack
Farm Hack has adopted the open source master frame in a more prominent way. Several aspects of the frame are highlighted both in all of the interviews and the Farm Hack platform, forum and other material. For instance, the Farm Hack culture section in the platform critiques the patent system as "most agricultural tools are built in a framework of proprietary knowledge generation—companies invest money in research and

development, and license their design in a way that does not allow others to replicate it, or even know how it is made" and offers the open source way as the solution: "the open source community believes that everyone benefits from freely sharing knowledge and working together to create new tools to fit our needs".

Similarly to L'Atelier Paysan, they have adopted a Creative Commons license for all the tools uploaded in the platform. They also use solely free and open source software acknowledging the division between the terms open source and free software which, according to an interviewee, finds Farm Hack somewhere in the middle (the practical application of open source and the political implications of free).

As far as the development process of hardware itself is concerned, Farm Hack has adapted the design principles outlined within the open hardware movement and expanded them to fit the agricultural production context. Hence, the Farm Hack principles may be condensed into an open source design model that is prioritising solutions that come from biological systems; includes personal gratification besides utility; uses standardised components or measurements and systems that simplify alterations and replication; is "transparent" (regarding the visibility of the tools' components); has modular components; is adaptable (tools to be used for more than one functions) and suitable for "disassembly", "replicability" and "affordability". Another set of Farm Hack principles, the community principles, feature several references to the open source frame such as a commitment to openly sharing knowledge and know-how; a lack of strict hierarchical forms of organisation and of the flexible open source structures; the use and promotion of collaboratively produced tools. These indicate strong commonalities with the open source development model promoted by several of the aforementioned movements under the master frame.

The interviews with members of the Farm Hack community reflect these views. According to Dorn, a strong motivation for the project "was to build a platform for knowledge exchange and a community that embraces the open source history of agrarianism" and "of course introducing the idea of copyleft right from the beginning". The community itself "has a strong framework and experience with the open source community functionalities" ranging from open source biofuel applications to software development according to Severine.

As Dorn points out, the decision to build the platform on Drupal was made due to several members' experience with the software. As for the tool developers contributing in the platform, their views also share the open source frame's principles. Interviewee A reflecting on the notion that humans have been sharing knowledge throughout history says that "the idea of withholding information for profit is new. It had a great run for 250 years where everyone hoarded their secrets trying to maximise their personal benefit but probably that's not going to be a permanent situation. All the open source movement is doing is to revive that previous state". Interviewee C, another farmer inventor, also points out that open source has been commonplace in history and while he would consider marketing his tools, he would never patent them. He believes that appropriate, reproducible, non-high technology is ideal for agriculture and that Farm Hack facilitates "open source, appropriate technology that can be skilled out in many places".

In general, the interviewees agree that Farm Hack has managed to bring attention to the application of open source in agriculture. In Dorn's words, "The original idea was to have a diversity of talents supporting agriculture. Roboticists; open source software community and really excellent farmers. To this extend we have been successful". But it did not end there. He adds that they were successful in "extending the idea of open source in agriculture from something really novel or odd into being not only accepted but expected. If you're not doing it you have a bit of explaining to do—there's a little bit of a social stigma, like you might be being greedy or short sighted. There has been a shift". Severine shares this view: "As a cultural project Farm Hack is very successful in normalising open source as desirable and empowering people to view themselves as potential designers", adding, "we were successful in making a cultural story about how a more open culture is an ancient tradition and proprietary, controlling uses of technology is ahistorical in agriculture".

However, she is critical of the way this story is framed: "the language and culture of software in the open source community has defined what the rules of open source are. It has limited the extent to which open source can penetrate the real world". Instead she argues for more focus on "the culture of a peasant—based movement, which is also open source. The passage of seeds and breeding technologies differs significantly from the way code migrates. Code and seeds are not the same thing". In a similar vein, interviewee C is somewhat critical of the strong focus on the open source software and its philosophy which potentially reduces the experience in the platform. He feels the focus of open source should be placed in the tool output rather than the notion of "open source everything".

It is evident that the open source master frame has been more prominent in Farm Hack with elements from all open source movements present, touching upon the development methods of open source software,
the design principles of open source hardware and the appropriateness of
tools. While it appears that some of these framings might be in conflict,
the overarching belief that knowledge should be freely accessible and technology should be appropriate and adaptable forms a unifying narrative.

4.2.2   The Organic Master Frame

Before industrial agriculture, all agricultural systems could be considered,
in one way or another, organic in nature. Scientific applications for the
manufacturing of farming inputs proliferated around Liebig's "Law of the
minimum" (van der Ploeg et al. 1999). This is basically the notion that
growth in plants is mainly determined by the scarcest element in the soil
(like phosphorus and nitrogen). This sparked the establishment of the
conventional agriculture science and industry with the synthetic creation
of nutrients that dramatically increased the productivity in crops (Goodman
and Redclift 1991).

The organic agriculture movement became prominent in the 1920s
with the work of Albert Howard in the UK and Rudolf Steiner in the
German-speaking countries. Steiner developed a set of lectures on biody-
namic farming, a system of organic agriculture, in response to the deterio-
ration of soil health and crops due to the use of off-farm inputs like
fertilisers (Paull 2013). He further established the "Agricultural
Experimental Circle of Anthroposophical Farmers and Gardeners of the
General Anthroposophical Society" to experiment with his methods which
greatly contributed to the emergence of organic agriculture (ibid.).
Steiner's work is akin to that of the Life Reform movement (Lebensreform)
which appeared in the late nineteenth century. Its activity focused on the
promotion of environmentalism, vegetarianism and rural living
(Vogt 2007).

Howard was an agricultural adviser in India where he was exposed to
various farming methods, mainly composting, which he then developed
further and promoted in the UK. Howard was critical of agricultural
research that aimed at profits rather that sustainability and practical farming (Hershey 1991). Howard's work inspired many, amongst which was
Lady Eve Balfour, an organic pioneer. In 1943, Balfour published her
seminal work *The Living Soil and the Haughley Experiment* that was the

first comparative study between organic and conventional farming (Balfour 1976). Following the success of her book in 1946, she cofounded the Soil association in the UK, an SMO dedicated to the goals of the organic movement which is still active today (Conford and Holden 2007).

Another important figure for the movement, Jerome Irving Rodale from the USA was so inspired by Howard's work, even though he was not a farmer himself, that he bought a farm to experiment with organic farming. Rodale published extensively, through his own publishing house, on the benefits of organic and the dangers (often unsubstantiated) of conventional methods (Kelly 1991). He also established an SMO, the "Rodale Institute", to promote the movement in the USA. The term organic agriculture itself is attributed to Lord Northbourne who first framed the farm as on organism in his book *Look to the Land in 1940* and soon came to be used extensively to describe non-conventional farming (Paull 2014).

During the 1950s, organic farming fuelled by its success in the UK and Germany was also popularised in France as "agriculture biologique" by Claude Aubert's work and the subsequent establishment of the "Nature et Progrès" association in 1964 (Vogt 2007). Over the next years, the movement successfully expanded in a global scale, and a multitude of local organic organisations emerged in the 1970s. In 1972, the International Federation of Organic Agriculture Movements (IFOAM) was established, an SMO coordinating the various independent initiatives and promoting the principles of organic agriculture.

The efforts of individuals, like the aforementioned, but also of farmers to provide alternative farming conceptualisations (for instance approaches like agroecology; permaculture; sustainable/biodynamic/regenerative agriculture) to the conventional ones led to the proliferation of communities and organisations promoting and developing these conceptualisations further. All these initiatives are aggregated in a movement under the organic moniker. It is hard to attribute a robust set of beliefs in the organic movement over the years, as there are various tensions and contradictions amongst the various approaches. The latter may range from a mere set of ecologically friendly methods to proposing a complete overthrow of the incumbent food production system (Guthman 2004). Yet the belief that agricultural activity within the profit-driven industrialised production is responsible for a range of unwanted effects constitutes a unifying force within the movement (Conford 2001; Guthman 2004).

This overarching critique of industrialisation in agriculture and subsequent turn into organic agriculture can be broken down into four movements and ideological framings that formulate the organic frame: (1) the agricultural production through alternative means, (2) the food and health movements, (3) environmentalism (4) and the counterculture movement that became prominent in the 1960s (Guthman 2004).

In 2005, the IFOAM published a set of principles revolving around health, ecology, fairness and care that frame organic agriculture. The principles were formulated through participatory processes by the members of the federation and were finalised in its general assembly (Luttikholt 2007). A brochure was produced and translated in several languages to disseminate the principles. The principles encapsulate the essence of the movement's history and influences as they were previously discussed here and may be viewed as motivational framing. After all, they have been labelled as the "ethical principles to inspire action" (IFOAM 2005).

Widespread market demand for organic food after the 1980s led to the adoption of organic methods and distribution systems globally (Aschemann et al. 2007). Originally sold in specialised vendors, soon major retail chains offered organic options boosting their popularity further. Organic regulations were established regionally to provide uniform rules for producers, notably in the EU, USA and Japan. These, however, led to increased costs to a developing industry, with the acquisition of an organic certification soon becoming a costly affair. Several European countries offered subsidies to support their national organic production as a result, though that is not the case with the USA where organic development is mostly market driven (Lohr and Salomonsson 2000; Uematsu and Mishra 2012). Further, market activity led to a concentration in production and consequently distribution. A result of both a dramatic growth of pioneering organic firms and the involvement of large conventional companies like McDonalds and Heinz (Aschemann et al. 2007). This meant that organic no longer meant local and fresh food necessarily. It was to tackle these rising concerns about the globalisation effect in organic farming that the IFOAM established the aforementioned principles.

Despite these efforts and the strict enforcement of regulations, there is evidence of what is called conventionalisation of organic agriculture. The organic farms are converted into the form of conventional ones since while their practices comply with regulations, they are not aligned with the principles of organic agriculture (Darnhofer et al. 2010). This conventionalisation takes place in various ways (Buck et al. 1997): through extensive marketing and the end of local food by distribution channels in a global scale; the abandonment of sustainable practices and adoption of intensive mono-cropping methods; substitutionism, the process of accumulating other food processing activities like packaging; appropriationism, meaning the process of externalising the various organic inputs traditionally developed in the farm like organic compost. This leads into a bifurcation between farmers, who are faithful to the organic principles, and organic producers, who engage in agricultural activity in the scale of conventional practices. This book explores communities whose organic farmers are squarely placed in the former category.

4.2.2.1 The Organic Master Frame in L'Atelier Paysan

The appropriation of the organic frame from L'Atelier Paysan is obvious. After all, as stated in the platform, it is "born out of an activist network of organic farmers in the Rhone Alpes region". Further, the platform states as a goal the promotion of organic practices through their tools: "the development of tools and self-built machinery adapted to small-scale farming is a technological, economic and cultural instrument which has been little explored within agricultural development in France, although it can provide a significant impact on the growth of organic farming and contribute to improving organic farming practices... For us, organic and small-scale agriculture go hand in hand. We cannot promote a model of organic farming which does not have a wider social vision behind it. Similarly, we believe that the principles of small-scale farming lead naturally to a chemical free approach".

The interviews illustrate the elements of the organic frame within L'Atelier Paysan. Indeed, the whole project began when Joseph adopted permanent raised bed technics more than 20 years ago. He says, "There were no machines in the market for this kind of system so we built them". Fabrice considers L'Atelier Paysan as part of the organic movement and in broader scale the ecology movement. He wants to engage in the debate for healthy eating and food systems as he believes that the conversation "should include tools for producing food as well as the open source agenda". Julien shares that belief and claims that his primary reason for his engagement in the project is "to tackle the challenge of how to feed humanity". He prefers the term agroecology over all other because it is more clearly defined and it reflects the practices they promote which are a step beyond organic, citing the use of green manure (a type of plant that nurtures the soil) as an example.

He continues, "If conventional farmers want to use our tools then that is very good but we will not adapt to their practices. These are practices of the past, not relevant at all for the future. We cannot afford them on an environmental or humane level". Instead, he says, their goal is to get them to convert into organic practices. Jonas, another member of the team, agrees: "Any farmer can join but our activity is quite specific and most of it is for small farms and organic agriculture".

Nicolas, whose background is in organic agriculture, is interested in collaborating with the various networks for organic agricultural development. Expanding on Julien's proposed practices, he says, "We have to choose a different agricultural model and we are trying to create it... we try to show farmers that our model is more accurate, relevant and diverse considering how agriculture and alternative agriculture work". He welcomes conventional farmers since he believes that if they want to use their tools then that means they, at least, are considering changing their practices. He says he wants to "make people think about how they farm through their machines... make them realise that there are other ways to do things". Etienne, one of L'Atelier Paysan's engineers who has become a peasant farmer himself, says that the very act of organic farming is political, meaning respecting the land rather than exploiting it, and he believes that most farmers working with them share this view.

Everyone agrees that the tools themselves carry the principles of the organic frame. According to Fabrice, they assist farmers in the making of simple and appropriate tools "but with a high level of agronomy". Joseph also prefers cheap, simple tools which are important for resilience. Because, while complex technologies are efficient, he thinks that "one day they might not be accessible. It is a possible scenario that one day we might not even have access to electricity. We need to diversify". He considers modern agriculture unsustainable because of its dependence on external inputs. This reflects the more radical environmental concerns within the organic frame.

The organic frame is adopted in a straightforward way by L'Atelier Paysan with a focus on the environmental benefits of these practices. While the term organic itself is used extensively, the group makes use of more precise language (like agroecology) to indicate approaches they promote which are deemed the most efficient and environmentally appropriate.

4.2.2.2 The Organic Master Frame in Farm Hack

The appropriation of the organic frame in Farm Hack is not as prominent, yet its elements are easily identified. According to the Farm Hack culture material, "Farm Hack aims to nurture the development, documentation, and manufacture of farm tools for resilient agriculture... By documenting, sharing and improving farm tools, we can improve the productivity and viability of sustainable farming". Resilient and sustainable practices are cited for a "healthy land" and "successful farms and local economies". The term organic agriculture is not employed even though, according to Dorn, the majority of farmers participating are organic producers.

A reason for not using the term organic is because Farm Hack is not limited to organic farmers but, according to Dorn, is "a community where the tools are a reflection of our understanding of the environment". Acquiring an organic certification is an expensive and complex process to navigate, and some farmers do not have it despite engaging in agriculture that could be considered organic. In fact, interviewee C suggests that organic standards are not enough. For instance, he says that the accepted rate of soil depletion considered sustainable is shockingly low. His critique goes further: "in the USA everything is about commercialisation and marketing and a lot of it gets green washed. There is a lot of co-opting and half-truths in that story- organic agriculture is sort of managed by the USDA (the federal agency for agriculture) and industrial organic has become pervasive. You can buy organic milk coming from a CAFO (concentrated animal feeding operation) that somehow manages to meet organic standards".

Interviewee B, a political science graduate and farmer, agrees that the USDA organic is usually problematic: "On the consumer level when people say organic they mean ecological but on the production level it does not necessarily mean so". He continues, "I am not against organic certification by any means but I do think it's only telling a part of the story, so I see the need for more precise definitions of sustainable agriculture". So, they deliberatively use more precise language about what practices they promote which may include "strictly carbon farmers or permaculturalists". This he says comes from "a desire to create an alternative system, a way to interact with the environment that is against the way industrial agriculture does". Interviewee C argues that for this reason "regenerative has emerged as agricultural methodology which might be better for earth but does not necessarily meet organic standards or actually surpasses them... we are trying to regenerate the soil and land base not just be 'sustainable' and depleting at a marginal rate".

Like L'Atelier Paysan, the tools themselves here also carry the organic frame, as Severine says, "Farm Hack is making clear the organic community's shared understanding of technology" since "there is this perception that if one is against farm inputs like pesticides and GM [genetically modified] then they are against technology and progress. Our point was to be more discerning—we are evaluating technology based on its cultural and ecological impact". "Ultimately it is not about the tool, it is about the agronomy", she concludes. Dorn adds that "it is about accessibility, ownership and scale with a discussion towards moving to biological systems rather than steel underlining it".

Interviewee A and his farmer brother believe that to create a sustainable food network, there will also need to be a local network that makes machines and solves problems for these farmers. That is because according to interviewee A, "Farming is a unique application of tools to environmental conditions, meaning that every farm has different conditions like soil type, altitude, rain fall etc. That means that every farm has unique technology problems that they need to fix". In a similar vein, interviewee C, who experiments on farm-scale perennial crops, builds the appropriate tools for the particularities of his approach. He says he leverages this technology to create an agricultural ecosystem which humans can maintain without the need of technology in the long-term. An approach similar to that of Joseph's which assumes a future worst-case scenario.

Several elements of the organic master frame have been adopted by Farm Hack, like the goals for environmental protection as well as sustainable and locally adapted practices, to tie together the various visions for alternative agriculture within the community. Institutionalised organic agriculture and mainstream organic narratives are criticised for their lack of substantial impact, focusing on scale and efficiency, and difficulty to navigate regulation-wise which limit adoption.

4.2.3   The Peasant Master Frame

While the organic movement evolved and expanded, ranging from promoting simple alternative farming methods to the conventional ones to suggesting the complete overhaul of the incumbent food system, the peasant movement pursued more politically focused goals framing its activity against the effects of neoliberalism.

The term peasant (amongst the equivalent terms are yeoman, campesino in Spanish and paysan in French) has been framed in numerous ways with further variations amongst geographical areas, yet often it carried a derogatory meaning. The term may signify social groups in the preindustrial industrial era that were legally bound, socially and economically inferior and considered subservient and "simple", while even today peasants in several areas in the planet lead deeply disadvantaged and precarious lives (Edelman 2013). The term may also describe communities with certain characteristics. For instance, peasants could be distinguished from farmers since the latter view their activity as an entrepreneurial project to be expanded, whereas the former aim merely to sustain themselves (Wolf 1966).

Even here, the definitions seem quite diverse and often interchange- able. A third way the term may be used is in an activist context, which is the connotation explored in this book. Having appropriated and empow- ered the term peasant, social movements give it a wider meaning to attract the maximum amount of constituents and adherents (Edelman 2013). La Via Campesina, arguably the largest transnational peasant movement which encompasses organisations from across the globe, defines peasants as people of the land (Desmarais 2007). Those that depend on and care for it, including those with little or no private land.

While contemporary peasant and agrarian movements rose into promi- nence in the late 1980s, they trace their roots further back, in the diverse and revolutionary attempts of peasants across the planet in a struggle to secure basic human rights and rural reform. Like the village population during the Mexican revolution in the 1920s that identified themselves as campesinos and demanded rural reform (Boyer 2003), or similarly the Bolivian revolution after 1952. In Europe, the peasant uprisings and agrarian parties were much grander in scale and activity. While their ide- ologies were quite different and often competing, there was common ground on the shared pursuit for the removal of landed groups and gen- eral land reform (Borras Jr. et al. 2008).

Jumping forward into the 1980s, we witness the rise of the several con- temporary movements following a major food crisis in a global scale. The reasons for this crisis were multiple: the massive increase in prices of fossil fuel (and fuel-based inputs) as well as other inputs like fertilisers during the late 1970s; the consequent rise in interest rates in combination with policies aiming to reduce inflation; the collapse of the Bretton Woods sys- tem which allowed the liberalisation and explosion of the globalised food trade; and as a result the fast decline of crop and livestock prices (McMichael 1998).

The domination of agribusinesses in all key agricultural sectors through chemical, mechanical and later biological inputs and the processing, stor- ing and exporting of basic food products enabled them to control a large part of the food market and influence agricultural policies in a global scale

(Edelman 2003; Kneen 2002; Lewontin 1998). These neoliberal reforms and the attempts to transfer the industrialised model of production, which would replace traditional systems in poorer countries (especially in the Latin America), has had a highly adverse effect in local peasant populations (Desmarais 2007).

It is within this socio-economic climate that peasant movements emerged in multiple regions across the globe. I discuss the movement of La Via Campesina, due to its role as an umbrella organisation, and the Confédération Paysanne, a French peasant SMO and leading actor in the peasant movement, both in France and globally, and a founding member of La Via Campesina.

The Confédération Paysanne emerged in 1987 out of leftist farmer groups that were unhappy with the French farmer's union (Fédération Nationale des Syndicats d'Exploitants Agricoles) and opposed the government's reform to modernise the agricultural sector which they claimed was marginalising small farmers. The Confédération Paysanne presented industrialised farming and globalisation as problematic and offered "peasant farming" (agriculture paysanne) as an alternative model of producing farm goods (either for commercial use or not) for the benefit of society (Morena 2015).

Peasant farming is framed as the opposite of entrepreneurial farming whose goal is profit maximisation and does not offer a specific set of practices to follow. It is not limited to certain farm size and could be organic or otherwise, yet it should respect the environment, food health and worker rights (Bove 2001). While originally the focus was set on criticising industrial farming for its obsession with productivism (deemed destructive for peasants), over time a more positive connotation was given to peasant agriculture that called for non-competitive, adaptive and autonomous activity (Morena 2014).

The Confédération Paysanne manifesto provides three principles attached to peasant farming: "it has a social dimension centred on employment, solidarity among peasants, among regions, among the world's peasants; it must be economically efficient by creating added value, in accordance to the means of production employed and volumes produced; it must be mindful of consumers while preserving the natural resources that it uses" (as cited in Morena 2014, p.3). This lack of specificity allows them to attach different meanings to match the various groups they are attempting to approach. According to the Confédération Paysanne, "peasant farming is neither a technique nor a model to follow or create, but an overall enterprise that involves all of a peasant's life and transcends the simple act of production" (as cited in Morena 2015, p.66).

In 1993, Confédération Paysanne cofounded La Via Campesina (translated as the peasant's way) along with several other peasant movements from Europe, Asia, Africa, Latin and North America. While cooperation existed before amongst the various movements, La Via Campesina was formed to offer global peasant coordination. It grew out of the previously discussed conditions in the last decades first by movements from third world countries, where rural populations experienced the worst side-effects of neoliberal and industrialisation/modernisation policies, and later from Europe and North America.

La Via Campesina uses a human rights frame to present their demands in various struggles, like land and resource enclosures, seeds, international trade and investments, in a common language that encapsulates the varying ideological, political and cultural flavours in the movement (Claeys 2014). These demands are distilled in the right to food sovereignty frame which was established in 1996 and over the years has been enriched, to address new issues like global warming and land grabbing, and are presented as the focal point of peasant struggle (ibid.).

Reports of La Via Campesina advocated ecologically resilient and autonomous practices applied by small, family and community-run farms (La Via Campesina 2010, 2013). A 2010 report states that there are multiple examples of peasant and family sustainable practices which might be called "agroecology, organic farming, natural farming, low external input sustainable agriculture, or others. In La Via Campesina we do not want to say that one name is better than another, but rather we want to specify the key principles that we defend" and "sustainable peasant agriculture comes from a combination of the recovery and revalorization of traditional peasant farming methods, and the innovation of new ecological practices" (La Via Campesina 2010, p.2). While in a following report, it is clarified that organic practices are imbued with the peasant ethos as "peasant based sustainable production is not just about being "organic"" (La Via Campesina 2013, p.9) since "industry is also appropriating so-called "organic food", so we need to differentiate between "industrial organic" and "peasant" or "family-farm organic"" (ibid., p.16).

4.2.3.1 The Peasant Master Frame in L'Atelier Paysan

Given that it is even in the title, the peasant frame is the most prominent one in L'Atelier Paysan. The organisation is also part of the La Via

Campesina and Confédération Paysanne networks. The critique of the agribusiness is evident in the platform: "In France, technological practices in agriculture are mainly driven by the agro-industry and correspond to its particular needs. This complex process is likely to continue, until farmers using these technological practices which are not tailored to their real needs, reassert ownership of the system-wide design of their farms". The solutions offered aim to enhance farmer autonomy and efficiency through the dissemination of farmer created tools: "we identify and document inventions and adaptations of tools, created by farmers who have not waited for ready-made solutions from experts or the industry, but have invented or tweaked their own machinery".

But also the collaborative development of new solutions: "we provide advice and guidance for small-scale farmers on agricultural tools tailored to their needs, and accompany them through their trials and tribulations in their farming journey, individually or collectively, whatever their area of production", and the training of farmers to achieve the capacity to manufacture themselves since "building a tool, farmers gain in autonomy as they learn metal work. A farmer who has built rather than bought his/her tool is better placed to repair or adapt it in future".

Adapting and expanding the narrative of food sovereignty, L'Atelier Paysan encapsulates their activity in what they call "technological sovereignty" for peasants. According to their advocacy documentation: "by promoting peasant autonomy through the reappropriation of knowledge and know-how around the farm production tool, L'Atelier Paysan promotes technological sovereignty of the countryside. We argue that it is the responsibility of the farmers to question their tools of work, machines and buildings, their financial, agronomic and ergonomic impact". This critique lies in the heart of the initiative and is reflected upon the tools they create: "we are careful with the tools that we agree to develop, and ensure that they respect the ethical principles of L'Atelier Paysan. We want to develop agricultural machinery which supports small scale organic farming, and which can be appropriated and modified by farmers" (translated from the French language by myself).

The L'Atelier Paysan members reaffirm this goal. Fabrice, while critiquing the agribusiness sector, says "I consider half of the industry tools inefficient. Their purpose is to support a financial system and often farmers buy tools they don't need because someone told them to… Unlike seeds and where their products are sold, there is no political critique about machinery in agriculture, yet historically the farmer is the machinery engineer and is sharing with other farmers... Now industry has taken over everything". Julien is also concerned about the concentration of equipment and seed markets in the hands of just a few big companies which are driven by their business models rather than the needs of the farmers. He expands his criticism to the supposed user innovation culture within the industry: "Even if it is contaminating big companies their goal is to make profit. This is not our goal, we don't pay our shareholders. We are not accountable for that—the only thing we are accountable for is our social goals".

Instead Julien says their goal is to promote technology that is affordable and easy to recreate, use and repair. Nicolas expands on that thought: "We promote, and help farmers build tools that are simple in conception and reproducible in the farm, with few materials and equipment. That is how we promote low investments, autonomy. That is how we make farmers independent from banks, agroindustry and make sure that they own their tools". Jonas views this as a highly political project. He says, "Self-construction means something politically. That you are not part of the commercial system and that's how you get more autonomy". He considers the type of technology they promote as important for farmers "because they have needs and with it they can cover them themselves". They have been quite successful in creating a positive view on self-construction according to Joseph, who cites a law passed in the French parliament that recognises it as the best way for farmers to be efficient. He says this development was heavily influenced by L'Atelier Paysan's activity.

As far as the workshops are concerned and the resonance they have had with the farmers in France, Fabrice believes the reason is the competitive nature of modern farming. The success of L'Atelier Paysan is partly explained by its appeal to new farmers who have no heritage in farming and are eager to learn. He says, "It is a nice metaphor of them constructing themselves as farmers". Gregoire, whose job is to assist the farmers in the creation of the tools and conduct the workshops, aims to remove barriers of competence and confidence "It is important for me to demystify the work of metal and machines themselves. A farmer that can work metal will be able to transform tools into something new. It is important for a farmer to have the confidence, if they have an agronomic idea and some knowledge of mechanical systems, to pursuit it". In the long term, he hopes that farmers will not require his expertise and L'Atelier Paysan will merely be providing logistics support while the "transfer of competence will be from farmer to farmer".

The peasant master frame provides substantial context for L'Atelier Paysan with strong references to farmer autonomy and sustainability. While the goals of contemporary peasant movements are fully embraced by L'Atelier Paysan, the food sovereignty framing has been extended to include technological sovereignty as the group deems it is often omitted in the debate within larger transnational peasant SMOs.

4.2.3.2 The Peasant Master Frame in Farm Hack

The peasant master frame is less prominent in Farm Hack than in L'Atelier Paysan even though according to Severine "Farm Hack is only possible because of the existing peasant network". However, she claims that the peasant language is not widely used in the USA. This partly explains the heavy focus on open source language software within Farm Hack despite the many similarities between the two approaches with regards to collaborative endeavours and open knowledge dissemination. Interviewee C believes that peasant mobilisation in the USA is small, underfunded and often defeatist. Regarding state support, he says, "It can be clunky as far as small scale agriculture is concerned because they're basically bought and paid for by large agribusiness interests". Interviewee B continues this critique: "It's a political analysis of where power lies in the system. In saying that power is held by giant manufacturers who can afford investing in research and development and lobby in the government".

Similarly, Kristen says that while engaging in small sustainable agriculture, "it became clear that farm technology is focused on industrial scale agriculture and there is a gap between what small farmers need and that is available on the market". So she and other farmers create their own creative solutions to their needs, yet she says, "It shouldn't just be up to farmers to solve their problems. Food is fundamental to our society and farming is a high-risk and challenging profession. I think the resources of our society should serve the purpose of growing food better and more effectively... and that is the case, but at one scale of agriculture only" (referring to industrial scale agriculture). Severine's views are even more radical. There are converging monopolies around basically four large companies with established innovation hubs, university accelerator programmes and government grants she says and concludes that "the militarisation of agronomy is the next phase in totalitarianism"!

While these peasant frame-driven views are held by people within the community, they are not voiced and featured prominently in the Farm Hack framing. According to interviewee C, a reason for that is that USA farmers suffer from "tall poppy syndrome" regarding their opinions and are afraid of being outspoken. Tim, who during our interview almost used a Marxist quote but did not quite complete it, says he does not use this type of language because people tend to think that it does not have practical applications. On not finishing the quote he says, "I guess I stopped myself because if you use that language here, the immediate response is 'so how are you going to make any money' and then you need to backtrack and say 'look, I'm not making any money anyway—I will never make any money because the market system does not allow it'". With Farm Hack, they are trying to "break out of the system and make something that should have been made before us and not ruining the planet at the same time". And the language used instead is based on rational arguments and examples that work with people Tim says, as illustrated by the Farm Hack platform.

The initiative is defined within the historical context of agrarian activity but with a focus on new farmers and new approaches developed in collaboration with allied social groups. Dorn feels there is a sense of continuity that comes from embracing the history of agrarianism which was open source: "It's not something we invented; we are continuing. We are part of something that has a much larger lineage… learning from the past but looking at the future", or "peasants of the future" as Severine calls it. According to Dorn, it goes back to the yeoman farmer ideals, the granges and agrarian politics which is "not class politics and it's not libertarianism"; he says, "It has the elements of independence and mutual aid, a non-commercial and a non-competitive market approach". On this continuity, Kristen compares the USA to Europe and says that the small farms never went away in Europe, while "in the USA it feels like we're re-inventing a lot of things". Dorn says they are imagining a yeomen's agriculture that is "diverse, direct to the market, with equipment that can be owned by the farmer or the community", yet like Kristen he thinks that to achieve this they need to invent the tools for it. But it is a big challenge with the greatest potential "to shift the mentality in order to have more empowerment at the farmer level" as Dorn says referring to convincing farmers to learn to build tools themselves or in the community rather than seek to buy them.

In general, there is a lot of overlap between the Farm Hack community and other collaborating organisations like those of the greenhorns and the National Young Farmers Coalition according to Dorn. So their politics spill over, like access to land, funds for education and healthcare and all things relevant to farmers being more successful and "having a more level playing field". The peasant frame is adopted in a wider, less obvious way in Farm Hack to appeal to as many constituents as possible. Hence, it focuses on the historical context of peasant agriculture and the capacity of the model in the modern world to address farmers' needs which functions as the driving factor for the wide range of views within the community.

4.2.4   Formulating the Open Source Agriculture Frame

I have distilled the various framing processes each of the case engage in into three master frames, which embody the common elements in the various social movements that produce them. The cases tap into these grander narratives and engage in frame alignment to concisely articulate their elaborate goals and various activities. While the individual case frames are not identical, there are commonalities to be systematised in order to articulate the new collective action frame shared by communities and individuals engaging in open source agriculture. A visual representation follows (Fig. 4.1), which illustrates the basic elements emerging from the data collected by either case. Combined they offer the central narrative of the frame.

To systematically represent the data, I employ three framing tasks, namely diagnostic, prognostic and motivational. Diagnostic framing involves the identification of a problematic situation and the attribution of blame. In this case, the three master frames are bridged to offer a multidimensional critique of the modern, conventional agriculture and the technology supporting it. The agribusiness sector is deemed responsible for the elimination of small- and mid-scale farms and traditional farming methods through the implementation of technology and practices that detach farmers from the land and cause great resource depletion and environmental destruction. The technology, supposed to assist the farmers into tackling their problems, is developed without their input and serves the interests of large companies. Farmers are either devoid of appropriate tools or unable to purchase the ones available in the market, due to patents that instead of protecting creators' rights are now perceived as a tool for profit maximisation. Governments and knowledge institutions, like universities and research centres, are often viewed as complicit in this hostile system.

The prognostic framing is also a synthesis of solutions promoted by each of the three master frames. Due to the nature of the open source

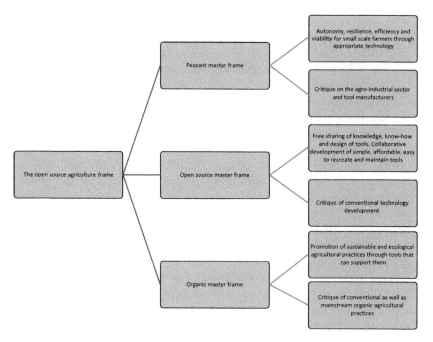

Fig. 4.1   The elements of the open source agricultural frame. (Source: Author's creation)

agriculture movement, that is, it being a technology and product-oriented movement rather than exclusively oppositional, the solutions offered are not in the form of demonstration and direct opposition but rather as alternative approaches to tackling their problems: technology developed by farmers for farmers with the assistance of designers, engineers and software developers. This type of technology is portrayed as truly suitable for enabling small-scale farmers to engage in alternative agriculture. The collaboration, the sharing of resources, knowledge and know-how amongst farmers is also promoted as a way of increasing viability and efficiency.

The motivational framing features the vocabularies of motive that are socially constructed to justify the movement's activity and spark further mobilisation. I have observed three motivational frames corresponding to each master frame. These are openness, sustainability and autonomy. Openness framing amplifies the merits of the open source model and collaborative processes as opposed to proprietary approaches that appear ahistorical and incompatible with agriculture. The open source model is presented as a natural continuation of ancient agricultural practices which were collaborative rather than antagonistic, while modern ICT technologies allow for such collaboration in a scale never before possible.

The sustainability framing pertains to the severity of the environmental and health concerns over conventional agriculture which for some is leading to certain collapse. Instead, it promotes systems that are good for the environment and provide healthier food. Or in the worst-case scenarios, "lifeboat" systems and tools which may be effective even under the most adverse conditions. These systems, while diverse in methods and approaches, are all viewed as radically different both in scale and philosophy from conventional ones since they refuse to treat the aforementioned concerns as externalities and they affirm the conviction to work with nature rather than impose on it.

Last, autonomy is presented as concerned with securing independence and resilience for farmers who are potentially contingent on a system that is beyond their control and does not cater to their needs and interests. Worse still, large companies are viewed as powerful enough to influence public institutions in order to assume control and manipulate the entire sector according to their own interests. The perceived solution is to break free from this system and operate as independently as possible. This may be achieved through minimising external inputs, self-creating machines and tools, diversifying the activities and skillsets of farmers and establishing collaboration and support networks.

In conclusion, the open source agriculture movement offers a critique of the incumbent system and a vision of technology attuned to socially and environmentally conscious agriculture which, according to its adherents, is posed to eventually replace it. The critique is distilled down to the essence of technology. In Fabrice's words, people in the agricultural production usually "are not interested in tools. I mean they are not thinking about the political implications of tools. But technology is political, it is not neutral. They see it as not political. Just technology, just progress. In this way nobody questions the technology. Talking about what we do opens another door as it is lack of visibility that allows this to happen. One piece of technology paves the way for one political goal, and another piece leads to another goal". The vision then is an amalgam of the elements from each master frame appropriated by the movement constituents which may be encapsulated as open source sustainable technology geared towards autonomy and resilience. Next I further explore this technological aspect of the movement to identify how the ideological proclivities and beliefs of the constituents, as well as the availability of resources and socio-political opportunities inform the nature and development process of the techno logical artefacts.

BIBLIOGRAPHY

Aschemann, J., Hamm, U., Naspettiand, S. and Zanoli, R. (2007) "Organic Markets", in Lockeretz, W. (ed) *Organic Farming: An International History*, Wallingford: CABI

Balfour, E.B. (1976) *The Living Soil and the Haughley Experiment*, New York: Universe Books

Benford, R.D. and Snow, D.A. (2000) "Framing Processes and Social Movements: An Overview and Assessment", *Annual Review of Sociology*, 26, pp. 611–639

Borras, S. Jr., Edelman, M. and Kay, C. (2008) "Transnational Agrarian Movements: Origins and Politics, Campaigns and Impact", *Journal of Agrarian Change*, 8(2/3), pp. 169–204

Bove, J. (2001) "A Farmers International?", *New Left Review*, 12, pp. 89–101

Boyer, C.R. (2003) *Becoming Campesinos: Politics, Identity, and Agrarian Struggle in Postrevolutionary Michoacán, 1920–1935*, Stanford, CA: Stanford University Press

Buck, D., Getz, C. and Guthman, J. (1997) "From Farm to Table: The Organic Vegetable Commodity Chain of Northern California", *Sociologia Ruralis*, 37, pp. 3–20. https://doi.org/10.1111/1467-9523.00033

CERN. (2017) *CERN Open Hardware Licence*, Available at: http://www.ohwr. org/projects/cernohl/wiki, accessed 17 May 2017

Claeys, P. (2014) "Food Sovereignty and the Recognition of New Rights for Peasants at the UN: A Critical Overview of La Via Campesina's Rights Claims over the Last 20 Years", *Globalizations*, Advanced online publication, https:// doi.org/10.1080/14747731.2014.957929

Conford, P. (2001) *The Origins of the Organic Movement*, Edinburgh, Scotland: Floris Books

Conford, P. and Holden, P. (2007) "The Soil Association", in Lockeretz, W. (ed) *Organic Farming: An International History*, Oxfordshire, UK and Cambridge, MA: CAB International (CABI), pp. 187–200

Darnhofer, I., Lindenthal, T., Bartel-Kratochvil, R. and Zollitsch, W. (2010) "Conventionalisation of Organic Farming Practices: From Structural Criteria Towards an Assessment Based on Organic Principles. A Review", *Agronomy for Sustainable Development*, 30(1), pp. 67–81

Desmarais, A. (2007) *La Vía Campesina: Globalization and the Power of Peasants*, London: Pluto

Edelman, M. (2003) "Transnational Peasant and Farmer Movements and Networks", in Kaldor, M., Anheier, H. and Glasius, M. (eds) *Global Civil Society*, London: Oxford University Press, pp. 185–220

Edelman, M. (2013) "What is a Peasant? What are Peasantries? A Briefing Paper on Issues of Definition", *Prepared for the first session of the Intergovernmental Working Group on a United Nations Declaration on the Rights of Peasants and Other People Working in Rural Areas*, Geneva

Elliott, M.S. and Scacchi, W. (2008) "Mobilization of Software Developers: The Free Software Movement", *Information Technology and People*, 21(1), pp. 4–33

Goodman, D. and Redclift, M.R. (1991) *Refashioning Nature: Food, Ecology, and Culture*, London: Routledge

Guthman, J. (2004) *Agrarian Dreams: The Paradox of Organic Farming in California*, University of California Press

Hatch, M. (2014) *The Maker Manifesto: Rules for Innovation in the New World of Crafters, Hackers and Tinkerers*, New York: McGraw-Hill

Hazeltine, B. and Bull, C. (1999) *Appropriate Technology: Tools, Choices and Implications*, Academic Press

Hershey, D.R. (1991) "Sir Albert Howard and the Indore Process", *Proceedings of the Workshop History of the Organic Movement*, pp. 267–269

IFOAM. (2005) *Principles of Organic Agriculture Preamble*, Available at: http://www.ifoam.bio/sites/default/files/poa_english_web.pdf, accessed 19 July 2017

Kelly, W.C. (1991) "Rodale Press and Organic Gardening", *Proceedings of the Workshop History of the Organic Movement*, pp. 270–271

Kneen, B. (2002) *Invisible Giant: Cargill and Its Transnational Strategies*, London: Pluto Press

Kostakis, V., Niaros, V. and Giotitsas, C. (2014) "Production and Governance in Hackerspaces: A Manifestation of Commons-based Peer Production in the Physical Realm?", *International Journal of Cultural Studies*, 18(5), pp. 555–573

La Via Campesina. (2010) *Peasant and Family Farm-based Sustainable Agriculture Can Feed the World*, Available at: https://viacampesina.org/downloads/pdf/en/paper6-EN.pdf

La Via Campesina. (2013) *From Maputo to Jakarta: 5 Years of Agroecology in La Via Campesina*, Available at: https://viacampesina.org/downloads/pdf/en/De-Maputo-a-Yakarta-EN-web.pdf

Lewontin, R.C. (1998) "The Maturing of Capitalist Agriculture: Farmer as Proletarian", *Monthly Review*, 50(3), pp. 72–84

Lohr, L. and Salomonsson, L. (2000) "Conversion Subsidies for Organic Production: Results from Sweden and Lessons for the United States", *Agricultural Economics*, 22(2), pp. 133–146

Luttikholt, L.W.M. (2007) "Principles of Organic Agriculture as Formulated by the International Federation of Organic Agriculture Movements", *NJAS—Wageningen Journal of Life Sciences*, 54, pp. 347–360

McMichael, P. (1998) "Global Food Politics", *Monthly Review*, 50(3), pp. 97–111

Morena, M. (2014) "Words Speak Louder than Actions: The 'Peasant' Dimension of the Confédération Paysanne's Alternative to Industrial Farming", Conference paper for at: *Food Sovereignty: A Critical Dialogue*

Morena, M. (2015) "Words Speak Louder than Actions: The 'Peasant' Dimension of the Confédération Paysanne's Alternative to Industrial Farming", *The Journal of Peasant Studies*, 42(1), pp. 45–71

Morrison, D.E. (1983) "Soft Tech/Hard Tech, Hi Tech/Lo Tech: A Social Movement Analysis of Appropriate Technology", *Sociological Inquiry*, 53, pp. 220–248, https://doi.org/10.1111/j.1475-682X.1983.tb00035.x

Nascimento, S. and Pólvora, A. (2016) "Maker Cultures and the Prospects for Technological Action", *Science and Engineering Ethics*, 24, pp. 927–946

Niaros, V., Kostakis, V. and Drechsler, W. (2017) "Making (in) the Smart City: The Emergence of Makerspaces", *Telematics and Informatics*, 34(7), pp. 1143–1152

Paull, J. (2013) "A History of the Organic Agriculture Movement in Australia", in Mascitelli, B. and Lobo, A. (eds) *Organics in the Global Food Chain*. Ballarat: Connor Court Publishing, pp. 37–61

Paull, J. (2014) "Lord Northbourne, the Man Who Invented Organic Farming, a Biography", *Journal of Organic Systems*, 9(1), pp. 31–53

Pearce, J.M and Mushtaq, U. (2009) "Overcoming Technical Constraints for Obtaining Sustainable Development with Open Source Appropriate Technology", *2009 IEEE Toronto International Conference Science and Technology for Humanity (TIC-STH)*, Toronto, ON, pp. 814–820. https://doi.org/10.1109/TIC-STH.2009.5444388

Perens, B. (1997) "The Open Hardware Certification Program", *Debian Mailing List*, Available at: http://lists.debian.org/debian-announce/1997/msg00026.html

Pursell, C. (1993) "Address Presidential: The Rise and Fall of the Appropriate Technology Movement in the United States, 1965–1985", *Technology and Culture*, 256(3), pp. 629–637

Raymond, E.S. (1997) *Goodbye, "Free Software"; Hello, "Open Source"*, Available at: http://www.catb.org/esr/open-source.html, accessed 16 May 2017

Raymond, E.S. (1998) "The Cathedral and the Bazaar", *First Monday*, 3(3)

Schumacher, E.F. (1973) *Small is Beautiful: Economics as If People Mattered*, New York: Harper & Row

Smith, A., Hielscher, S., Dickel, S., Soderberg, J. and van Oost, E. (2013) "Grassroots Digital Fabrication and Makerspaces: Reconfiguring, Relocating and Recalibrating Innovation?", *SWPS 2013-2*, Brighton: SPRU

Soule, S.A. and King, B.G. (2008) "Competition and Resource Partitioning in Three Social Movement Industries", *American Journal of Sociology*, 113(6), pp. 1568–1610

Stallman, R.M. (2002) *Free Software, Free Society: Selected Essays of Richard M. Stallman*, Cambridge, MA: GNU Press

Uematsu, H. and Mishra, A. (2012) "Organic Farmers or Conventional Farmers: Where's the Money?, *Ecological Economics*, 78, pp. 55–62. https://doi.org/10.1016/j.ecolecon.2012.03.013

van der Ploeg, R.R., Bohm, W. and Kirkham, M.B. (1999) "On the Origin of the Theory of Mineral Nutrition of Plants and the Law of the Minimum", *Soil Science Society of America Journal*, 63, pp. 1055–1062. https://doi.org/10.2136/sssaj1999.6351055x

Vogt, G. (2007) "The Origins of Organic Farming", in Lockeretz, W. (ed) *Organic Farming: An International History*, Wallingford: CABI

Willoughby, K.W. (1990) *Technology Choice: A Critique of the Appropriate Technology Movement*, London: Intermediate Technology Development Group Publications

Wolf, E.R. (1966) *Peasants*, Englewood Cliffs, NJ: Prentice Hall

Zelenika, I. and Pearce, J.M. (2011) "Barriers to Appropriate Technology Growth in Sustainable Development", *Journal of Sustainable Development*, 4(6), pp. 12–22

CHAPTER 5

Technology Matters

Abstract This chapter expands on the technology theories utilised in this book, namely the social construction of technology and critical theory of technology. After reviewing each, the chapter offers a synthesis of the two that builds on the results of the social movement analysis. Specifically, it merges two specific concepts of frames, collective action frames from social movement theory and technological frames for technology theories. The emergent frame translates the values of the former into technical specification for the latter.

Keywords SCOT • Critical theory of technology • Alternative technological trajectories

Technology permeates every facet of the social structure. Chapters 3 and 4 discussed open source agriculture through a social movement framework, exploring what mobilises those involved in these initiatives. Primarily their activity revolves around the design and fabrication of technological artefacts that enable the participating individuals and communities to pursue their goals. Here, I use a different set of theoretical approaches, focusing on the study of technology to further explore this activity. There is a plethora of research approaches and philosophies of technology making sense of its intertwining with society. So, this book is inevitably selective with the approaches used to tackle the phenomenon under examination.

© The Author(s) 2019   69
C. Giotitsas, *Open Source Agriculture*, Palgrave Advances in
Bioeconomy: Economics and Policies,
https://doi.org/10.1007/978-3-030-29341-3_5

This chapter presents a synthesis of these approaches and how they incorporate the results from the analysis so far. Before that, I offer some context as even the very definition of technology is wide and contested. What we understand as technology determines what the focus for research should be as well as its basic assumptions and limitations.

5.1   WHAT IS TECHNOLOGY?

The term "technology" has been used for surprisingly little time dating back to, possibly, the seventeenth century and was only widely used in the late twentieth (Nye 2006). Until then, the term technics was employed to describe collectively the "tools, machines, systems and processes used in the practical arts and engineering" (ibid., p.12). Etymologically the word is derived from the ancient Greek "techne". Greek philosophers, like Plato and Aristotle, distinguish nature ("physis"), which perpetually re-creates itself, from "poiesis", which is the human activity of creating an artefact (Feenberg 2005). Techne describes the knowledge and principles relevant to a certain type of poiesis, like for instance carpentry or ironwork. Nowadays the term is more complex with the various academic disciplines and approaches providing definitions for "technology", "technique", "science", "technoscience" or "society and technology" according to their specific foci of analysis.

Early twentieth century philosophers of technology, like Martin Heidegger and Jacques Ellul, have built on the Greeks' conception of technology, seeking to strip away the contextual layers and pinpoint the fundamental essence of technology (Dusek 2006). This essence was often viewed as rather harmful for the human society since it was perceived as beyond human control and detrimental for community and spiritual values (Brey 2010). This view was also shared by the advocates of critical theory like Marcuse, who considered modern industrial technology as having imprisoned humans in a destructive consumption cycle. However, Marcuse adds, the goal should be to conceive a technology embedded with social and environmental values. This updates the notion of techne from its ancient Greek meaning, imbuing it with the capacity to reorganise modern society.

Scholars from the science, technology and society tradition adopt a more practical and precise approach to defining it. Technology may be perceived in three levels: technology as artefacts, like mobile phones and computers; processes or activities, like designing the mobile phone; and knowledge around technology (MacKenzie and Wajcman 1985). This last level corresponds to the ancient Greek definition and entails the information and know-how regarding the manufacturing, use and maintenance of a certain piece of technology.

Technology is often misunderstood as applied science. Science aims to produce models and theories that provide insight for phenomena. The term technoscience is often used, illustrating how theory and practice—science and technology—have become too similar (Misa 2009). While the boundaries between the two are becoming ever more blurry, technological artefacts often precede scientific exploration or even make it possible (Nye 2006). Throughout human history tools were developed before a scientific explanation existed for what they do and how, though cutting-edge technology nowadays usually involves both. Within this book, the boundaries are clearer as the individuals and groups, upon which it is structured, view technology as artefacts and processes that may be created and re-created by the users themselves. While the scientific community and experts are often sought after, their role is assistive, and the focus is placed on the tacit knowledge and experience of the users, that is, the farmers whose day to day activities and needs spark the creative process for a new technological artefact.

Contemporary technology theorists, like Andrew Feenberg and Don Ihde, influenced by the empirical focus in the study of technology in the 1980s have abandoned their predecessors' pursuit of that single essence. They argue that technology is too complex and broad to be distilled in a single subject (Dusek 2006). Feenberg (2003) specifically, as a student of Marcuse and proponent of the critical theory school of thought, notes that there is a gap between macro-level philosophical analyses of technology and empirical research, which needs to be bridged. This book is informed by this insight, and while it is built on these broad theories, it attempts to explore the notion of alternative technology through the multifaceted study of the two communities and their technology development models.

5.2   THE STUDY OF TECHNOLOGY

Technology as a theme is researched within various fields. Since I cannot review all approaches in this book, an overview is presented to situate this work within the fragmented terrain. The broadest distinction of narratives underlying the study of technology is between technological determinism and constructivism. A second layer placed upon this distinction may be between the aforementioned macro-level, philosophical (and often, at least perceived as, deterministic) critiques of modern technology as a whole; and empirical (predominantly constructivist) studies in the micro- and meso-level, which explore individual artefacts or systems of technology. Below, I elaborate on this distinction and formulate the synthesised setting within which technology is dealt within the book.

5.2.1   Technological Determinism

The study of technology has been dominated by determinism (Dafoe 2015). Technological determinism is built on the belief that technology is independent of societal influence and its progress is fixed. Instead, societies adapt to technological progress to facilitate the requirements of each new piece of technology. In this sense, the development of new technology does not take place within society and thus does not consider societal factors. This stance has excluded technology from humanistic studies since its explanation lies in technical rationality and scientific discovery rather than a social interpretation.

While the definition above describes the simplified version of technological determinism, there is still debate as to what truly constitutes determinism. It is also referred to as "hard" by scholars. In another form of determinism, identified as "soft" or "mild", technology is perceived as a driving force for social change but influenced by social, economic, political and cultural factors (Smith and Marx 1994). Twentieth century technology philosophers like Jacques Ellul, Lewis Mumford and Martin Heidegger are viewed by many as soft determinists and pessimistic against technology which they deemed was out of human control. This can possibly be attributed to the fact that since the beginning of the century heavy industrialisation caused severe social and environmental degradation, while technology has been widely used for warfare (Brey 2010).

Ellul (1964) posits that technology has become an autonomous system that advances itself through social structures and values that place efficiency and logic above everything else, to the detriment of spiritual and moral values. Lewis Mumford (1966) similarly speaks about the mega-machine that "assembles" human beings to do its bidding. Their views led them to ascertain that the solution to the problem of modern technology might be to be rid of technology altogether. While some (Fores 1981) treat these views as soft determinism, others believe them to be critiques on the socioeconomic system that creates this technology rather than the technology itself (Wyatt 2008).

Wyatt classifies determinism based on the perception of certain social groups and individuals. These are descriptive, methodological, normative and justificatory (Wyatt 2008). Descriptive is the form used by technology theorists as a form of identifying and avoiding it in their work. Methodological determinism is employed by other theorists to examine the role of technology within society by placing it in the centre of their investigation. Normative determinism argues that technology has become so big that it is no longer under societal control. Last, justificatory determinism is the one deployed by societal actors and can be found everywhere around us, from policy documents to corporate decision-making. It is the type of deterministic rhetoric associated with the common views regarding technology and employed to justify controversial decision-making under the pretext of unavoidable technological progress.

Technological determinism, in its justificatory variety, is the most problematic, and while it has been vilified by technology scholars as simplistic and devoid of political agency, it is widely shared among social actors, and hence merits attention. That is because it still informs the popular opinion and decision-making processes regarding technology (Wyatt 2008). Determinism persists because technology is so pervasive in human societies that it is easy to mistake it as the only driving force (Heilbroner 1994). Its simplicity then is probably the reason why it persists. It corresponds with most peoples' experience with technology, that is, adapting to new pieces of technology whose design process and manufacturing remains largely a mystery (Wyatt 2008). It just makes sense. This is important in the context of this book because, unlike those who welcome determinism as an excuse to uncritically consume new technology, the members of the communities explored are keenly aware of how technology affects their lives. They reject this predicament and strive to produce technology aligned with their values.

That is noteworthy because agriculture is a sector where technological determinism has dominated the narratives of development. Determinist discourses have allowed agribusiness to push the capitalist, industrial logic of agriculture that was seemingly technologically determined and consumer driven (Hamilton 2014). Technological determinism was the façade used to justify the inevitable introduction of large-scale mechanisation as an external input to heavy agriculture in the name of unstoppable technological progress.

Yet this technological shift was far from apolitical or independent. It carried the logic of the free market and the interests of large vertically integrated corporations, which made the deterministic view of inevitable technological progress towards that direction a self-fulfilling prophecy (ibid.). It follows then that the political impact of the groups examined in this book should be significant considering that they do not adopt a technophobic stance against technology and consequently reject it all together. Instead they aim to build an alternative narrative; one that enables critical appraisal and more democratic decision-making regarding new technology.

5.2.2   Social Construction of Technology

On the opposite side of determinism is the social constructivism of technology. The latter is built on the premise that technology is socially constructed and is influenced by a plethora of economic, political and cultural factors as well as the interactions of the various groups involved in its development. That is not to say that technology does not have a profound effect in society, but rather that it is not fully autonomous or neutral.

The field's origins go back to the sociology of knowledge tradition that regards knowledge in general and science facts as socially constructed. While this notion has been criticised extensively, its application in technology is less controversial as there are no metaphysical elements to contest. Technological artefacts are constructed after all. Constructivism in technology was popularised in the early 1980s, following the proliferation of empirical studies regarding technology that can be aggregated under the "social construction of technology" (SCOT) or the "social shaping of technology" title, but also "actor network theory". They examine technology not with a capital "T" but rather as individual technologies or technological systems (Bijker et al. 1987).

These approaches rely on the premise of symmetry. Symmetry implies that failed cases of technology are of equal capacity for insight concerning technological and social issues and should be examined symmetrically. Its application to technologies studies is exemplified by the dispelling of the myth of objective technical superiority for the advancement of certain technologies over others (Bijker 1997). This means that, at any given time, there is always more than one technical solution for a specific problem and the prevailing one is not necessarily the most efficient, but it depends on the social environment that enabled its dominance. Essentially all actors, human or not, involved in the process of technological development are to be treated as having the same level of power to influence it. The SCOT approach, which is the least conceptually and methodologically hazy, preserves the duality of society and technology and posits that technology is the one determined by society.

While the SCOT framework has mostly been used as an approach within historical analyses of emerging technologies, it may also be used as a tool for the sociological study of technology (Bijker 1997). Similarly in this book, technology is explored as a snapshot of its evolving development. Pinch and Bijker (1987), who popularised this approach, introduced the notion of relevant social groups as the basic social units involved in the development of technologies. They may be institutions, organisations or simply groups of individuals (organised or not) which share a similar interpretation of a technological artefact. These social groups identify certain problems and corresponding solutions during the development of new technology. Different social groups ascribe different problems as relevant in the process, thus affecting the form of the technological artefact. While an individual may be part of more than one relevant group, each one has a unique interpretation of the artefact.

Since the various groups view the technological development of a technology differently, there is interpretive flexibility in the way an artefact evolves, which means that there is not just one artefact but as many as the relevant interpretations. Interpretive flexibility is another SCOT concept to track how problem solving regarding a technology differs amongst relevant groups (Pinch and Bijker 1987). The interpretive flexibility of an artefact demonstrates the various meanings imbued to it by the groups. An artefact is not merely technically developed but affected by social conditions. Bijker exemplifies this in his study of the bicycle's history, where various versions existed concurrently satisfying the needs of different social groups, instead of it evolving linearly as is usually assumed (Bijker 1997). Over time the multiple versions of the bicycle diminished as a result of interaction amongst social groups, leading to gradual stabilisation and closure in the version everyone is familiar with today.

Stabilisation and closure are two more useful concepts of SCOT. Stability is achieved when the relevant social groups negotiate and align their interests in a certain iteration of the technological artefact. As the meanings attributed to the artefact begin to homogenise, it gradually stabilises. After several renegotiations, a dominant design will be accepted by all groups and closure will be reached. A black box state where no further changes may take place. The artefact becomes obdurate and its essence fixed, with all previous controversy around its form disappearing. It follows then that the final product is not necessarily the most efficient or successful version of the artefact but rather the outcome of all the aforementioned social interactions leading into consensus.

SCOT adopts an extreme approach in the constructivist account of technology, which might be considered social determinism (Bijker 2010). Thomas Hughes' technological systems offer a milder approach, bridging the two extreme versions of determinism. Systems are defined as amalgams of political, economic, social and political components beside the technical ones. The basic tenet here is that technological systems gain momentum as they grow and become more mature (Hughes 1987). This is due to various factors that constrain the social shaping of technology like established infrastructure and standards; sunk costs and fixed assets; people employed and routines; and embedded interests. While their origins are indeed social, these limitations are not designated by certain groups and can therefore be perceived deterministic in nature. Technology is always socially determined in its conception, yet over time technological determinism sets in. Such are the automobile and electric power systems which still hold considerable momentum in our contemporary circumstances, though systems do decline and eventually get replaced like the gas lighting and the canal transportation ones that preceded the aforementioned.

Bijker, building on the systems approach, proposes another unit of analysis, calling it a sociotechnical ensemble (Bijker 1997). Those with a high level of inclusion have a broad range of flexibility and options within the ensemble they are embedded in, but it is almost impossible for them to operate outside of it. Those with a low level inclusion, on the other hand, experience a "take or leave it" dilemma. Should they choose to take it, they have very limited capacity to influence the ensemble, but if they choose to leave it, then it is possible for them to thrive outside it.

Viewing modern agricultural technology as either a technological system or a sociotechnical ensemble, a clear parallel can be drawn with the technology examined in this book. Agribusiness companies dominate the system and shape it according to their interests. Farmers engaging in large-scale agricultural production enjoy a high level of inclusion and are able to navigate it and prosper. Yet they would not be able to support their activity outside of it due to their heavy dependence on external inputs and highly mechanised methods. Smaller actors, on the other hand, like the ones featured here, are practically not included. It is almost impossible to appropriate this technology for alternative uses. Yet it is relatively easy for them to exist outside of it.

Admitting that social groups cannot simply conceptualise and create technological artefacts without any restrictions, Bijker (1995) introduces the concept of technological frames. Frames as conceived in SCOT are not purely cognitive structures, but contain material and social elements as well, and are used by analysts to structure data under consideration and track interactions within social groups (ibid.). They do not describe characteristics of individuals or institutions, but are the glue that binds the actors together. They offer the problem as well as possible solutions but limit the freedom of the actors within them.

A technological frame emerges when work around an artefact begins. It organises the interactions amongst individuals in social groups, formulates their thinking and practices but also limits their capacity to design radically new technologies (Bijker 1995). There are as many frames as social groups around an artefact and individuals might be placed in more than one frame. The concept itself is broad enough to focus on different elements depending on the case it is applied in and for it to be applicable not only to the technically savvy (like engineers) but also all to other individuals within social groups (Bijker et al. 1987). It is comprised of all the components that lead into the attribution of meaning in artefacts. Those components might include (but not be limited to) the following: "goals, key problems, problem-solving strategies (heuristics), requirements to be met by problem solutions, current theories, tacit knowledge, testing procedures, and design methods and criteria" (Bijker 1997, p.123), but also other, previously established obdurate artefacts, cultural values, user practices and perceived substitution elements.

There are three possible configurations for technological frames within a sociotechnical ensemble: "when no clearly dominant technological frame is guiding the interactions, when one technological frame is dominant, and when more technological frames are at the same time important for understanding the interactions related to the sociotechnical ensemble that is being studied" (Bijker 1993, p.128).

In the first configuration, usually in effect during the early stages of technological development, there are no established frames as there is no dominant social group and perhaps several radical artefacts. Success is dependent on the formulation of a strong frame with the enrolment of several allies that will direct resources along a certain trajectory. The next configuration is dominated by one group and frame that is strong enough to articulate both the problem and the solutions to address it, limiting the range of technological solutions within the ensemble. The last configuration is populated by several competing technological frames, with varying problematisations and solutions. External factors are paramount for the technological choices made in this configuration, and the interests of all groups will be accounted for in the technological output.

Following the earlier parallel, the agricultural sociotechnical ensemble is dominated by the large-scale, highly mechanised and chemical input-intensive technological frame as in the second configuration. The frame allows those with high inclusion to define which problems are to be tackled and with what solutions. Those with a low level of inclusion are kept outside the development process and adoption through excessive costs and strict intellectual property rules that prohibit them from appropriating and adapting the technology. The only viable option is to cooperate and establish a competing frame that will account for their interests and goals as they were articulated in the previous chapter.

Iacono and Kling (2001) studied technological frames that, much like collective action frames in social movement research, were employed to mobilise adherents, demobilise possible antagonists, elicit resources and support in order to achieve certain technological developments. They focus primarily on goals, prognostic and diagnostic processes, theories, user practice and existing artefacts. Their conceptualisation of technological action frames provide a reasoning for the adoption of a technology which encompass shared understandings, expectations and beliefs on how the technology works. It also includes master frames rising over competing frames and stabilising the discourse around a certain technology through a specific set of meanings.

I follow a similar line of reasoning where the aggregated frame of the open source agriculture frame is translated into the technological action frame for the movement which itself shapes the technological output of the two cases. The next section explores the theory enabling the consideration of political and normative aspects of technology but also ameliorates the shortcomings of the constructivist approaches as even though they have the capacity to contribute to the political critique of technology, they are constrained into the examination of specific technologies. In other words, they do not expand into the broader political bias, which may influence the entire network of actors or social groups involved in the development process. While the very notion that technology is socially driven may be viewed as political, they tend to offer descriptive accounts of how technology emerges rather than offering any criticism or normative evaluation about its place in society (Winner 1993).

5.2.3   Critical Theory of Technology

A critical theory of technology investigates the economic, political, social and cultural values that motivate the production of technology in order to make normative assessments on the function of technology in society. Contrary to most constructivist research, which focuses on the nuances of their empirical work and is wary to expand beyond it, this approach does not shy away from broad generalisations about technology practices and cultural values from carefully selected indicative cases. Through these cases they "show the ordering, disciplining, rationalizing and modernizing processes that are associated with technology" (Misa 2008, p.372). An epistemological and methodological conflict appears at this point (ibid.).

It is possible, however, to bridge the two approaches and formulate a comprehensive theory on technological change based on empirical evidence (Feenberg 2003). This multilevel view is the foundation that informs the empirical aspect of this book and provides a connection to the wider socio-political context influencing both cases. The social movement framework is used to provide a reconciling methodological element between the perspectives of individuals and groups acting autonomously and the birds-eye point of view for the structural whole, which transcends the limits of the empirical case studies.

The notion of power is central in critical theories of technology that examine how technology is used to influence its distribution in society. Technology allows actors or social groups to exercise power with the use of technological artefacts and systems by either providing them with new powers or by allowing them to exercise existing power more effectively than others. People can be coerced, seduced, forced, manipulated or simply expected to respect a specific authority through certain delegated technological artefacts (Brey 2007).

However, there are instances of resistance amongst social groups at the receiving end of asymmetrical power relations. Critical theories serve the normative goal of seeking better ways for power to be resisted and distributed more symmetrically in society through technology which is the primary focus for this book also. A more democratic, just and free version of technology is understood as constituting a foundation for better distribution of power in society (Brey 2007). The democratisation of technology, meaning the wider participation of the public in its development and use, is a topic that several technology theorists have tackled (see for instance Winner 1986; Feenberg 2002)

The most prominent example of a critical theory of technology is offered by Feenberg, who provides a thorough overview of technological change and the politics that drive it in modern capitalist society. Feenberg's critique of technology developed within the capitalist production system is focused on its concern with securing profit and power. As Marcuse's student, he draws his inspiration from the Frankfurt school but, like Marcuse to some degree, rejects their grim outlook against technology as an instrument of domination. Instead he envisions change that stems from activity at the micro- and meso- levels by the marginalised who acquire the consciousness, and subsequently the technologies, to do so despite having to contend with much more powerful opponents like global corporations (Feenberg 2002).

5.2.3.1 Indeterminism, Technological Hegemony and Technical Codes
Regarding research on technological systems, Feenberg proposes indeterminism, instead of unilinear determinism, whereby technological development follows technological branches that may reach a high level on more than one track. Such development is not a determining factor for society but is rather overdetermined by social and technical factors alike. To illustrate the flexibility of systems over social pressure, he provides the example of child labour and work hours in the nineteenth century (Feenberg 2002). Machines, at that time, were designed to account for a small person's frame and a factory was organised to function in a back-breaking rhythm. It was a fact of life, technology demanded it. Initially, requests for regulation with (partial) elimination of the former and reduction of the latter were met with fervent resistance based on the imperatives of technology. A multitude of alarming "technical" counter-arguments were offered around the reduction of efficiency (narrowly defined within that specific paradigm) and competitiveness, increase of inflation and ultimately economic collapse. However, once regulations were placed, not only this was not the case but efficiency increased and the system gradually adapted to and internalised the new social conditions into its guidelines and practices. Looking back child labour is considered a non-issue, the reconfiguration of the system seems inevitable and the social struggles that took place are largely forgotten.

On the other hand, when one looks at the future, it is quite difficult to conceptualise technologies to tackle societal issues that exceed the restrictions of current technological configurations. As Feenberg puts it, "not only is it difficult to anticipate future technical arrangements, it is all too easy to think up utopias that cannot be realized under the existing ones" (Feenberg 2002, p.98). That is because technological design is limited by economic, political and cultural factors often employed by powerful social groups to dominate over the rest. The prevailing capitalist technological rationality is imprinted into the technical base of society through a form of social hegemony that reinforces a hierarchal structure by selecting certain technological configurations over others. The assembly line, for instance, exemplifies how control through enforced repetitive and low-skill tasks around machinery is employed to increase productivity and profits for the management rather than improve the well-being of the workers (Braverman 1974).

All this is made possible by incorporating the aforementioned social factors in the technical design, language and practices through a process Feenberg calls instrumentalisation (Feenberg 2008). Instrumentalisation takes place in two levels. Primary instrumentalisation breaks down technological artefacts into their most basic elements, decontextualising them from the social environment. There, one can observe the most rudimentary of social influences, and distinguish which physical and technical principles are most important. However, during the secondary instrumentalisation, these elements are re-contextualised in the social world, and values, meanings and goals are coded within and influence the ultimate design of new artefacts.

These "technical codes define the object in strictly technical terms in accordance with the social meaning it has acquired" (Feenberg 2002, p.88), and much like technical culture itself, they remain largely unseen and self-evident. Only through careful investigation can one uncover the controversies that have taken place during their formulation. Hence, new iterations of mainstream technologies, like a car or a tractor, must conform to certain codes in order to be accepted in society at any given time. Yet the establishment of these codes over others was the result of conflicting ideologies and interests with the most powerful social forces defining the technical rationale shaping these technologies.

Technical codes dictate the design and manufacturing of technologies; the processes to be followed; standards and guidelines to adhere to in order to achieve maximum efficiency (broadly defined by private economic interests and ignorant of all other side effects which are largely socialised). In this sense, technical codes define many aspects of social life, but rather than treating them as containing some sort of deterministic capacity or functional rationality, we may trace historically certain social interests attributed to and calcified in them. Similarly, the technical codes defining modern agricultural technologies are largely concerned with maximising yields, usually in large-scale applications and ensuring, of course, continuous profits and control for their manufacturers. But they are not expected to consider environmental arguments or the demands for the autonomy and well-being of small-scale farmers. So they safely ignore them.

5.2.3.2 Democratic Rationalisation

This version of critical theory is meant to expose the underlying technological rationality in society and provide support to those initiatives that seek to be mobilised around radical new technologies. In other words, to uncover the formal bias which, although it appears neutral or devoid of values with a mere focus on efficiency, structures systems in such a way so as to serve the interests of certain social groups. To this end, Feenberg (2002) promotes what he calls democratic rationalisation which re-examines basic assumptions and values that are self-evident, both in the technical code and the relevant social structures and institutions. According to this notion, a democratised technology is not only achieved through the participatory design of new technological artefacts, but also through the alternative re-appropriation of existing technology as well as social movement resistance and protests, which push for shifts in the technological paradigm.

Micropolitics then, in the form of protest, participatory design, innovative dialogue and creative appropriation, bring issues about technology to the fore and open up its definition as something more than mere tools for profit and power. Feenberg (2002) offers the example of environmental controversies that mobilised ecological networks whose protests have managed to bring attention to those affected. This movement ultimately did influence the technical codes embedded in certain industries to, at the very least, recognise environmental concerns and liability to those responsible. He further provides examples of technology transfer (especially of agricultural technology) initiatives in third world countries which proved unsuccessful for the most part unless they involved local communities in the design process. Last, he provides the case of the French Minitel as an example of individuals re-appropriating technologies. While originally introduced as an information distribution component accompanying home telephones, users quickly began using it for anonymous chatting thus transforming it into a communication device. Feenberg stresses the capacity of micropolitics in which individuals engage in collective action, inspired by suppressed values like race and gender equality, ecology and meaningful work, to challenge the impact of the dominant technological rationality (Feenberg 1999).

Similarly, as I explore in the next chapter, in the case of open source agriculture, those technological externalities like environmental conservation or even regeneration, sustainable development and quality of work for smaller farms—which are largely ignored over concerns for wield efficiency and profit maximisation—become points of contestation for those who realise alternative potentialities through technologically mediated activities. In other words, individuals sharing the same values aggregate locally, but also on a global scale through ICT, to materialise their technical needs and promote an alternative technological rationalisation.

Yet Feenberg questions the emancipatory potential of the movements he has explored, as they could be perceived as simply facilitating society's further enrolment to the existing technological logic. Initiatives from below often succeed in influencing the incumbent technical rationality without radically altering or destroying it as their political demands are negotiated (or even coopted) and translated into "technically rational terms" (Feenberg 1999, p.90). Whether the initiatives explored in this book and other similar ones will be able to lead the way for radical change in the underlying technological rationality remains to be seen. At least, however, they boast a mixture of the elements discussed by Feenberg, along with a unique understanding of the technological factors' impact in their activity and interests. After all, there is a long history of agricultural technical systems structured on different codes than the contemporary ones. Furthermore, farmers are the ones most proficient in their field, based on extensive experience with natural systems and tacit knowledge developed and disseminated in farmer to farmer networks over generations.

BIBLIOGRAPHY

Bijker, W.E. (1993) "Do Not Despair: There is Life After Constructivism", *Science, Technology & Human Values*, 18(1), pp. 113–138

Bijker, W.E. (1997) *Of Bicycles, Bakelites and Bulbs*, Cambridge, MA: MIT Press

Bijker, W.E. (2010) "How is Technology Made?—That is the Question!", *Cambridge Journal of Economics*, 34(1), pp. 63–76

Bijker, W.E., Hughes, T.P. and Pinch, T. (1987) *The Social Construction of Technological Systems*, Cambridge, MA: MIT Press

Braverman, H. (1974) *Labor and Monopoly Capital*, New York: Monthly Review Press

Brey, P. (2007) "The Technological Construction of Social Power", *Social Epistemology*, 22(1), pp. 71–95

Brey, P. (2010) "Philosophy of Technology After the Empirical Turn", *Techne*, 14(1), pp. 36–48

Dafoe, A. (2015) "On Technological Determinism: A Typology, Scope Conditions, and a Mechanism", *Science, Technology, & Human Values*, 40(6), pp. 1047–1076

Dusek, V. (2006) *Philosophy of Technology: An Introduction*, Wiley-Blackwell

Ellul, J. (1964) *The Technological Society*, New York: Vintage Books

Feenberg, A. (1999) *Questioning Technology*, New York: Routledge

Feenberg, A. (2002) *Transforming Technology: A Critical Theory Revisited*, New York: Oxford University Press

Feenberg, A. (2003) "Modernity Theory and Technology Studies: Reflections on Bridging the Gap", in Misa, T., Brey, P. and Feenberg, A. (eds) *Modernity and Technology*, Cambridge, MA: MIT Press

Feenberg, A. (2005) *Heidegger and Marcuse: The Catastrophe and Redemption of History*, New York: Routledge

Feenberg, A. (2008) "From Critical Theory of Technology to the Rational Critique of Rationality", *Social Epistemology*, 22(1), pp. 5–28

Fores, M. (1981) "Technik: Or Mumford Reconsidered", *History of Technology*, 6, pp. 121–137

Hamilton, S. (2014) "Agribusiness, the Family Farm, and the Politics of Technological Determinism in the Post-World War II United States", *Technology and Culture*, 55(3), pp. 560–590

Heilbroner, R. (1994) "Technological Determinism Revisited", in Smith, M.R. and Marx, L. (eds) *Does Technology Drive History? The Dilemma of Technological Determinism*, Cambridge, MA: MIT Press, pp. 67–76

Hughes, T.P. (1987) "The Evolution of Large Technological Systems", in Bijker, W.E., Hughes, T.P. and Pinch, T.J. (eds) *The Social Construction of Technological Systems*, Cambridge, MA: MIT Press

Iacono, S. and Kling, R. (2001) "Computerization Movements: The Rise of the Internet and Distant Forms of Work", in Yates, J. and Van Maanen, J. (eds) *Information Technology and Organizational Transformation: History, Rhetoric and Practice*, London: Sage, pp. 93–135

MacKenzie, D. and Wajcman, J. (1985) *The Social Shaping of Technology*, Milton Keynes: Open University Press

Misa, T.J. (2008) "Findings Follow Framings: Navigating the Empirical Turn", *Synthese*, 168, pp. 357–375

Misa, T.J. (2009) "History of Technology", in Berg Olsen, J.K., Pedersen, S.T. and Hendricks V.F. (eds) *A Companion to the Philosophy of Technology*, Oxford, UK: Wiley-Blackwell

Mumford, L. (1966) "Technics and the Nature of Man", *Technology and Culture*, 7, pp. 303–317

Nye, D. (2006) *Technology Matters: Questions to Live With*, Cambridge, MA: MIT Press

Pinch, T.F. and Bijker, W.E. (1987) "The Social Construction of Facts and Artifacts: Or How the Sociology of Science and Technology Might Benefit each Other", in Bijker, W.E., Hughes, T.P. and Pinch, T. (eds) *The Social Construction of Technological Systems: New Directions in the Sociology and History of Technology*, Cambridge, MA: MIT Press, pp. 399–441

Smith, M. and Marx, L. (eds) (1994) *Does Technology Drive History*, Cambridge, MA: MIT Press

Winner, L. (1986) *The Whale and the Reactor*, Chicago and London: University of Chicago Press

Winner, L. (1993) "Upon Opening the Black Box and Finding it Empty: Social Constructivism and the Philosophy of Technology", *Science, Technology and Human Values*, 18, pp. 362–378

Wyatt, S. (2008) "Technological Determinism is Dead; Long Live Technological Determinism", in Hacket, E.J., Amsterdamska, O., Lynch, M. and Wajcman, J. (eds) *The Handbook of Science and Technology Studies*, 3rd edition, Cambridge, MA: MIT Press, pp. 165–180

CHAPTER 6

Open Source Agriculture: An Alternative Technological Trajectory?

Abstract Here the two subcases are reviewed under the theories expanded upon in Chap. 5. Again either subcase is reviewed independently first and then comparatively. Analysis takes place on both micro and macro levels. Ultimately, the technological action frame of the movement is compiled that is utilised to provide certain insight on the nature of the technology produced by the movement. Specifically, the impact of values as well as societal factors in the shaping of the technology itself.

Keywords Technological action frame • Farm Hack • L'Atelier Paysan • Interpretive flexibility • Technical codes

It is now time to examine the cases as hubs of technological development, whose particularities are important towards alternative conceptualisations of technology. I treat L'Atelier Paysan and Farm Hack as technological communities, beside SMOs, to illuminate the productive aspects of their activity. To do so, the technology development model of both cases is examined using the conceptual tools presented in Chap. 5. The movement's collective action frame formulated in Chap. 4 is translated into the technological action frame that provides the guide for the shaping of technological artefacts in each case. I expand on the resource mobilisation inquiry of Chap. 4, focusing on technology. This helps establish what effect socio-economic opportunities and limitations have on technology. In addition, I consider the political and cultural environment in each country to account for their differing effect in each case. These elements provide the complementary building blocks for that translation. Last, I incorporate the effect of the wider socio-economic context on the organisational form and development model in each case focusing on the role of the state.

6.1   Technology Development and Organisation Model

This section sketches out the processes taking place for the aggregation, development, improvement and dissemination of technological artefacts in the two organisations. I discuss each case individually to address the intricacies of their respective approaches.

6.1.1   L'Atelier Paysan

L'Atelier Paysan employs a robust structure to both aggregate farmer-developed technologies and collaboratively produce new ones marrying the rich peasant (tacit) knowledge with novel approaches of design and manufacturing. Furthermore, L'Atelier Paysan engages in critical thought building around technology which permeates all their activities. The term "technologies" does not simply imply farming machinery but also specialised processes as well as building infrastructure to accommodate these processes.

I provide here an overview of the L'Atelier Paysan model, pieced together through a series of interviews with individuals working for the organisation; multimedia material mostly available openly through the L'Atelier Paysan website and forum but also graciously provided by the organisation; and my attendance in the annual gathering of L'Atelier Paysan, which featured several workshops as well as two tools: a cereal brush and a seed drill. These on-site visits form the narrative basis for this overview as they illustrate the most important aspect of L'Atelier Paysan's activity, the collaborative design and fabrication of new tools. This allows for the exploration of the intricacies behind the L'Atelier Paysan development model through appropriate narrative cues.

6.1.1.1 Cereal Brush[1]

The first tool is a machine that removes the husk off cereals but also contributes to the reduction of mycotoxin (produced by fungi) levels, concentrated in dust. Its inception took place in the beginning of 2016 after ARDEAR, a peasant farmer association from the Rhône-Alpes area, approached L'Atelier Paysan. As Alexander, the association's representative in the workshop, explained to me a group of bread farmers were interested in acquiring a tool like that. Yet market options were too expensive and incompatible with their smaller volume of production. Hence, L'Atelier Paysan was brought in to help them develop their own tool, which would be suitable for their needs (which, in this case, is better quality of flour).

The first meeting with L'Atelier Paysan provided the basic parameters on what was needed by the tool. According to Nicolas, the ideal set of participants for the development of a new tool includes farmers, L'Atelier Paysan itself and a relevant organisation skilled both "technically and agronomically on the question we want to answer". The organisation not only would facilitate the process more methodically but would also coordinate the farmers to actively participate in the development process.

Then, research was done for materials and methods of processing cereals through contemporary machinery. Moreover, inspiration was drawn by similar tools created decades ago to conceptualise the basic design (since simplicity is paramount). The fact that potential patents for these tools have expired long ago adds to this choice even though regarding infringement "in agriculture everybody does it" according to Nicolas. That is because it is very difficult to prove something is new and unique when it comes to farming tools.

Furthermore, the legislation is grey in this regard. For instance, they devised a process to create the component for a star-shaped weeding tool cut by disposed material, inspired by a market tool typically made through injection in a mould. In this case, the patent was obvious due to the shape, Nicolas says. The creator of this component warned L'Atelier Paysan that they would take legal action since they considered this a patent infringement. However, several interviewees have said that, following the advice of a farmer in the L'Atelier Paysan coop who used to be lawyer dealing with this type of cases, they do not believe they would lose in court since

[1] All the relevant info for manufacturing the tool can be found here: https://www.latelier-paysan.org/Semoir-de-semis-direct-pour-cereales.

they are not selling or profiting with the tool or its designs. They considered proceeding with the case in a very public manner to bring attention to the lack of a clear legislative framework for the self-construction of tools but also challenge the legal (and technical) codes behind what constitutes a public good regarding technological artefacts. As Fabrice puts it, their solution is easily reproduced with do-it-yourself means, and it is agronomically efficient—"there is no reason not to appropriate it". Nevertheless, they deemed that it was not the right timing as they are "still too small". So instead, they altered the shape of the component to resemble the design of a similar one whose patent had expired.

Old designs then as well as several email exchanges with the farmers provided enough technical specifications for an early 3D draft of the brush tool. A second meeting took place in the L'Atelier Paysan central office, three months later (March 2016) to further refine the design. Six of the several farmers in the group were present (as not everyone is always available due to time and location limitations) as well as a collaborator of L'Atelier Paysan who manufactures small-scale artisanal mills. Technical elements, concerns and the desired features were discussed. Out of the various possible solutions for technical problems, the ones focusing on ease of implementation, adjustment and balancing were selected. Furthermore, the various empirically attained tips and tricks of everyone in attendance were implemented in the design. The wheat is to be funnelled in a cylindrical tube where a spinning rotor equipped with two steel brushes and two fins will process the wheat. An outer case allows for the collection of the dust and its disposal via a conventional vacuum cleaner.

This is a complex piece of machinery using electric power which, according to Joseph, probably reaches the limit of sophistication the group can aim for. He believes that the tools they develop should be simpler and easier to reproduce, yet he acknowledges that their role is to assist and possibly guide the farmers rather than indicate to them how they should be doing things. "We have worked with farmers to build big machines because this is what they wanted", he says, and adds that "a lot of people happy for it, so why not". He finds them unsatisfactory, however, due to their difficulty to adapt and use. This opinion is echoed by Fabrice who, while he admits that he is not against high technology (pointing to his smart phone), he opposes "technology that makes people just operators". He explains: "There are a lot of tools today were you just have to drive, not think. More and more farmers are not walking the earth, touching the soil... there is no more savoir faire (a capacity for appropriate action), autonomy or human interactions".

This could reflect the older generation's lack of familiarity with modern electronics technology but also their desire to create low tech tools, which would be reproducible with the most easily accessible material and the simplest possible processes. This, for Joseph, would create an invaluable library of technology suitable for a collapse of the current system, which he finds possible to transpire given the absolute dependence on external inputs that might not be there in the future. As for high tech machinery in the farm, he wonders "what happens in two or three years when the machine breaks?" Fixing it would require knowledge that farmers do not have. He adds, "People can use high tech machines but they need to be conscious of their dangers... we need to preserve farmers' independence, autonomy, resilience".

The relatively younger people on the community though, which features several new farmers whose background is in the ICT industry, recognise the dynamic of contemporary open source hardware technology. This is exemplified by the decision to facilitate Arduino microcontroller workshops for farmers to be able to use them in their activities (like using them in combination with sensors to measure greenhouse temperature and moisture levels). The rationale for this change, according to the call for participation, is that in order for the farmer to be the agent of technological development and to be able to recognise "the constraints and benefits inherent to each technology", they need to attain the necessary skills to use and innovate with them as long as they are easily appropriable. By having a basic knowledge of the technologies, they would be equipped to make informed decisions as to whether these technologies are suitable or not for their practices. This reflects the view of the group regarding technology and its impact on user autonomy. As Nicolas says, "When we speak about technology we don't speak about autonomy and that's a problem... right now farmers are not skilled in coding" and that limits their control over how electronics can influence their activities.

Let us now return to the tool. A date was set in the following month for the prototyping workshop. The details over fees were to be handled by ARDEAR. These include attendance and consumable (like electrodes, drill bits, cutting discs) costs. As previously discussed, most French farmers are eligible to tap into specialised funds for vocational training which cover for most of these expenses. During the workshop, three prototypes were to be constructed, each of which were to be later acquired by farmers provided they cover for the materials. The total cost is calculated at around 1000 euros, out of which 400 is the typical cost for a generic motor.

This workshop took place in a fabrication space rented by an agriculture school as a lot of farmers were expected to participate. Everyone arrives early in the morning and gathers in a classroom above the workroom where Etienne provides the specifics of the workshop and also discusses the L'Atelier Paysan approach to tools. The space below is already equipped with metal working tools, yet Etienne arrived with the L'Atelier Paysan van carrying all the necessary equipment and materials. In the course of two days, 13 farmers attended the workshop. All of them either experienced or novice bread peasants (paysan boulanger), most members of collective farms, whose activity ranged from simply making and selling flour to artisanal bread and pasta. According to Etienne, in practical terms, peasant usually connotes farmers involved in all aspects of a products cycle. For instance in this case, these farmers grow, harvest, store, process organic wheat and ultimately sell bread either in the farmer's market or in their farms. Etienne finds the term beautiful and something to be proud of. After doing internships in farms himself, he now aims to become a full-fledged cheese peasant (paysan fromager).

In general, there are typically three points in the workshop process. First, studying the blueprints which are created with much detail and in a step by step fashion, second cutting, drilling, welding components, and third assembling. The farmers change into the appropriate work attire and help set up the equipment. They then gather around for an introduction while handbooks with detailed instructions for metalwork as well as prints of the schematics are distributed. The design schematics and a list of tasks are set on the board which includes a table for everyone to note down as they rotate to the various steps and tasks. According to Etienne, as the facilitator of the workshop, he needs to maintain a good balance between the experimentation—fabrication and educational aspects.

Next, there is a demonstration of how to properly use the machinery and a general safety overview before the works begin. The farmers split into smaller groups and take up specific tasks while familiarising with the equipment. Some of the older farmers are more experienced so they provide assistance to the rest. Some worked as engineers for a few years before deciding to become farmers. Etienne moves around providing guidance and soon the work intensifies with the board being the focal point.

Lunch breaks are an opportunity for socialising and community building so everyone is expected to bring some food to share. Most bring home-grown vegetables, cheeses and other products they produce and sell, allowing them to exchange tips and ideas. I was asked in advance to bring something "English" as I was living in the UK at the time. Not being British myself, I brought some award-winning pork pies and some samosas (from my favourite Indian restaurant). They were well received I thought.

After the break, the intense work resumes which involves a lot of trial and error. Certain milestones of the fabrication process draw the attention of everyone. For instance, when the assembly is about to begin, Etienne gathers everyone around to participate. Everything is discussed thoroughly in order for all to be able to comprehend the process fully. Whenever a significant problem appears, everyone assembles again to brainstorm and collectively offer possible solutions. After about 12 hours of work, the first day of the workshop comes to an end having constructed the bulkier components of the three prototypes.

Since most of the farmers are based far away, they all spend the night together in the dormitory of the facility. This presents another opportunity for socialisation and knowledge exchange. Younger farmers have the opportunity to learn from the more experienced ones. Being peasant farmers is hard work and requires a lot of resilience. It is like having ten jobs in one according to Etienne. So they are used to collaborating and depending upon each other. He thinks the reason why the development process of this tool was easy is because the farmers were able to coordinate very well.

The second day of the workshop begins early with everyone resuming with the prototyping process, focusing on the finer elements of the tools. The main components of the tools are starting to receive their final form as the assembly process is about to begin.

By late afternoon the tools are taking shape, and as the workshop reaches its end, everyone makes an extra effort to complete their work. When another problem appears, everyone gathered around once more. A module does not seem to fit well and with not much time left to tackle the issue they resolve to finalise the process in the next meeting. Having reached the final stage, everyone is understandably somewhat disappointed.

Last, everyone works to clean up the workspace, gather the tools and go through the required paperwork and financial arrangements. A date for a second meeting is set. Three of the participating farmers will be taking the tools. Only at a fraction of the price of market options which would not suit their needs anyway, given that they operate in smaller scale than what these alternatives are designed for. The rest of the farmers claim that the reason they participate is to acquire valuable fabrication skills, which will enable them to make and improve the tool at a later time but also maintain and repair their current equipment. Most also confirm that they joined in the spirit of collaboration and sharing knowledge—this is how small-scale farmers always operated anyway.

The fabrication process was later finalised, and a second working group was set up in the Grand Ouest branch of L'Atelier Paysan, which built on this experience. A new prototype was manufactured, which validated the assembly and adjustment choices. However, the brushing of the tool was considered too aggressive by the farmers of the second working group. The current version of the schematics for the tool can be found in the "under development" section of the platform. A tested and validated version will be published in the main tool list once feedback from the prototypes is collected and the current form of the tool approved by all farmers. Nevertheless, this list does not offer final versions of tools created. Instead, farmers are constantly encouraged to adapt them to suit their needs and share their modifications with the community.

6.1.1.2 Seed Drill[2]

Activity for this artefact began in the autumn of 2015 after a presentation of the L'Atelier Paysan approach for tools in a farmer expo. Several farmers were interested in developing a large seeding tool suitable for no till farming (which is a method of growing plants without disturbing the soil and the microorganisms living within it and increasing water retention). A meeting with Etienne to discuss the possible tool took place in Francois's farm, one of the four farmers who were eager to proceed. They are cheese farmers and the tool would help them seed (primarily with sorghum, though it can be used for legumes and is also currently tested for cereals) their fields for their goats to graze on.

A second meeting was arranged in another farm a few months later to decide on specifications. Several email exchanges with technical points and initial designs took place in the meantime. The tool, there, has its final form validated. The basic elements include a row of discs, a row of teeth, a row with lead and grader chains, two triangle hitches (front and back) for extra versatility when mounted in a vehicle. And last a proprietary,

---

[2] All the relevant info for manufacturing the tool can be found here: https://www.latelier-paysan.org/Brosse-a-ble.

electrical seed distribution, ventilation and dosage detection system modified to be mounted upon the tool. Developing such a component from scratch is deemed too complex and costly by L'Atelier Paysan. Furthermore, according to Gregoire, certifications for that type of technical systems are difficult to attain adding that "every tool must be suitable for fabrication with cutting, drilling and welding. But some, more complex parts cannot be made like this".

Each of the tools L'Atelier Paysan develops comes with a folder of self-certifications for specifications and other issues like safety standards and insurance. For instance, they are allowed to use basic hydraulics with their current certifications, but cannot develop electrical systems or PTO (a method of receiving power from a different source, typically from a tractor in agriculture). These limitations in certifications are congruent with those prohibiting farmers from repairing their equipment, as illustrated by recent "right to repair" initiatives (of which Farm Hack is also part of) which highlight the lack of autonomy and the potential impact in farmer livelihoods. This is exemplified by the company John Deere, which prevented users from tinkering with the software embedded into their modern tractors, allowing only their dealers and their certified technicians to make repairs.[3] The long waiting period for these technicians to be available would potentially be catastrophic for farmers should a malfunction appear during periods of high activity. In both instances, the arguments defending this practice are ensuring the optimal performance of the systems and safety concerns.[4] Yet one could argue, following Feenberg's assertions, that these technical and legal codes are the result of the embedded monopolistic interests of manufacturers seeking profit maximisation through the exclusion of others in the technology development and repair processes.

Going back to the tool, after further debates regarding the design for fabrication is finalised and produced by Etienne. A date is set for the prototyping workshop in April 2016 (prototyping workshops usually take place in spring or summer and dissemination workshops take place in winter corresponding to the workload of farmers). Three days in La Roque-d'Anthéron, a rural area in south France, with the works taking place in a

---

[3] http://blog.farmhack.org/tag/ifixit/.

[4] See the letter against a, now passed in certain states in the USA, proposed legislation that will allow users to repair digital electronics. This is met with fervent opposition by not only agricultural machinery companies but also large electronics manufacturers like Apple and Microsoft as it may set a precedent: http://bit.ly/2BvOqHw.

large storage shed. I attended this workshop, and Francois was gracious enough to host me in his family farm along with two L'Atelier Paysan members, Etienne who would facilitate the workshop and Julien who joined for support and as my guide of sorts.

Etienne arrived with the L'Atelier Paysan van carrying certain prefabricated components of the machine beside the tools necessary for the workshop. These were pieces of metal that could only be shaped with industrial grade machinery. As Etienne told me, several of the tools they develop have such components, hence the designs come with detailed instructions for steelmakers to follow. A farmer, who was previously an engineer, also pointed out that some of the prefabricated parts would probably cost more and be less precise if self-fabricated instead of ordered. These specific ones were made by a metalwork professional who works closely with L'Atelier Paysan. I later had the opportunity to meet him in the L'Atelier Paysan annual gathering where he was presenting a small seeder tool of his own conception inspired by another tool created by some of L'Atelier Paysan's collaborators.

This workshop is atypical as the farmers were few and already quite adept with fabrication processes. While they all took turns familiarising with all steps of the process, a lot of improvising and experimentation was taking place as the various bits of the puzzle fit or not. As the day progressed, more farmers joined in. They were younger, relatively inexperienced farmers there to develop skills which would help them establish sustainable farms themselves.

After two days of intensive work, the tool is complete. Its total cost is calculated at about 5000 euros while market equivalents are priced upwards to 20,000 (and not optimised for the same use either). The four original farmers are to pay for the materials and keep the machine that they will use collectively. This tool is also in the under-development section while it is being tested in various applications by the farmers. According to Etienne, a part broke during its use, but having acquired the necessary skills, Francois was capable to repair it himself.

6.1.1.3 Annual Gathering

The cooperative's general assembly coincides with a big open gathering each year which is a celebration of their philosophy and progress. In 2016, it took place in a large collective farm over the course of three days with many workshops, discussions, exhibitions, music gigs and other events. This was their most ambitious gathering to date, according to Joseph, with significant resources of the cooperative directed towards planning, infrastructure and promotional material.

The gathering starts with the general assembly of the L'Atelier Paysan cooperative. A series of presentations regarding the previous year's activities take place. Then new members are introduced and voted in and the objectives for the next year are voted upon as well. There is little debate amongst the members, and they seem to put great faith in the operational team led by Fabrice and Joseph. Only one member is purposely absent from the proceedings. I am told that he finds it too business-like and calls for even more participatory processes led by farmers themselves (however later on, when he led a discussion about time management in farms, I tried to discuss his views with him, but he was hesitant to express any objections saying that the coop is doing a great job).

Several other discussions took place during the three days of the gathering ranging from the possible expansion to the use of open source software, seeds and patent use in agricultural machinery to body awareness exercises to help with the physical impact of farm work. The most engaging of these discussions are the ones sparked by independent groups presenting their own tools which they developed to tackle the unique requirements of their activity. Each group highlights the specific values and interests that drove the development process.

Workshops are organised around the estate, facilitated not only by L'Atelier Paysan but also by their collaborators broadening the scope into agronomical applications (like a wooden seed cleaning tool), raw material processing (like a self-built oven), introductions to microcontroller technology, energy production tools (wooden wind turbines) and other farm-related topics. Knowledge transfer takes place in all activities through experiential means. For instance, even the art workshop, where an artist collaborator of L'Atelier Paysan is demonstrating how sculptures can be created with repurposed scraped metal, is providing attendees with valuable metalworking skills.

The highlights of that year's gathering, however, were the building construction development projects and workshops that L'Atelier Paysan has been expanding to. Jonas, as the group's first resident architect, spent long hours visiting about 60 farms to study how farmers structure them in order to suit their specific type of activity best and making blueprints which are made freely available along with similar efforts by farmers themselves. Samples of these blueprints were put on display in the main venue of the gathering in order to emphasise another element of farmer ingenuity that is often overlooked.

Workshops are being planned, as well, for farmers to conceptualise new buildings with an architect's assistance or to develop their woodworking skills, typically while constructing a building on site. Jonas explains: "For mobile or modular constructions we rent a space to make it and then put it together like a puzzle in the farm... if the construction is fixed in a precise topography we do it in the farm". Regarding the importance of this expansion in activity, the relevant announcement proclaims that "when considering the question of adapting farm tools, the agricultural building is not separable from the equipment. That is why, after having invested ourselves on the question of adapted machinery, L'Atelier Paysan wishes to accompany the peasant dynamics with critical reflection and self-construction of their buildings. Because as much as farm machinery, the building is responsible for the proper functioning of the farm" (translated from the French language by myself). Through critical reflection, they encourage farmers to question their buildings, to think about the multiple functions they must fulfil and to consider their evolution over a long time from the moment of their installation.

It is easy to notice how buildings are developed with the same design principles as the machinery. Modularity, for instance, is a key aspect of open source technology, and the same is strived for here as well. An interesting example is the bati20. A highly modular, multipurpose, construction which can be modified to be used as a storage, living or commercial space. As its name implies, the original design's size is 20 m², but due to its modularity, it can be increased to whatever size the farmers need while its ease of assembly enables mobility as well. Another example is the mobile chicken coop which is an agronomic system tailored to organic peasant farming. As the coop is moved around the chicken clean up the soil. But as Jonas points out, it also eliminates the need to thoroughly sanitise the coop every time new chickens are to be introduced (which is the case for static coops). This one can simply be moved to different position. The goal is always to provide assistance in the technical and construction aspects, as farm buildings are quite specialised and farmers know better what they need.

What differentiates small-scale, self-constructed farm buildings from other constructions, according to Jonas, is that they are not as dependant, at least creatively, on building regulations and technical specifications. This provides farmers with relative freedom to construct buildings that are simple but very specific to their needs with locally sourced and often repurposed materials. He does, however, admit that they too need to get permissions, and in some cases, it is quite difficult. For instance, the bati20 is specifically set on 20 m² because up to this size no permits are required. Deciding to build a larger construct adds a layer of complexity which, while L'Atelier Paysan offers some advice for, is up to each farmer to deal with.

Once again, the technical codes embedded in these regulations come at odds with alternative conceptualisations of technology or, as Jonas puts it, with the "farming soul" as they enforce an approach that is too generic and without consideration of the local conditions. This is even evident in infrastructure development funding schemes some of which are subsidised in the EU level through its Common Agricultural Policy. The specifications for these are designed according to advanced and large-scale agricultural activities, typically taking place in western European countries, which demand significant financial resources and are incompatible with alternative systems of agriculture (especially in smaller, less technologically savvy countries in southern and eastern Europe). The infrastructure L'Atelier Paysan creates, on the other hand, is adaptable to the space, landscape and above all the type of activity taking place in each farm. Much like everything the group is involved with, the design files and all pertinent information regarding these buildings are fully documented and available for everyone to access.

As part of the gathering workshops, a mobile pigsty was constructed over the course of the three days which is based on the original design of a farmer's construction. A detailed overview, along with drawings and photographs, for the farmer's design can be found in the L'Atelier Paysan forum, the documentation for which was curated by Jonas himself. A large percentage of the blog posts are initiated by the L'Atelier Paysan operational group in fact. Lack of tech literacy amongst farmers is not a primary reason according to Fabrice, as many have basic computer skills and some even have a background in ICT. Other members attribute this phenomenon to the hectic work schedule of farmers, while Fabrice believes that another important reason is the fact L'Atelier Paysan provides a lot of assistance in all stages, which makes farmers less pro-active. At any rate, Julien admits that they do not have a concrete plan to tackle this issue, though the engineers do promote the use of the forum during the workshops.

The iteration developed by Jonas is an improved version designed in a standardised manner in order for it to be easily reproduced. It is ideal for farmers with pasture areas to move the sty (along with the pigs) in various locations depending on the type of farming employed. This system allows for the pigs to live comfortably while roaming freely but also for the soil to be prepared and enriched by their activity throughout the seasons. The design approach and ergonomics of this construction are aligned with those of all the other artefacts discussed before. During the event, the project was constructed from scratch enabling participants not only to acquire metalwork skills but also woodwork under the guidance of Jonas.

The gathering ends with the arduous disassembly of the event's infrastructure, for which several participants volunteered to assist, and a comedic auction of several sculptures created during the event. In a discussion with Joseph at dinner after all the work is done, he reveals that he was happy with the result even though the event consumed a lot of resources, time and energy. After all, they knew in advance that whatever proceeds they gathered, it would not be enough to break even. However, it was a testament and a celebration of the progress L'Atelier Paysan has achieved over the years, and he was convinced that it reached a lot of people.

6.1.2   Farm Hack

As illustrated in Chap. 4, Farm Hack's goals and vision are similar and, in some aspects, identical to those of L'Atelier Paysan. But their organisation and development model are in many ways quite different. The highly decentralised and to a large degree online activity of Farm Hack means that engaging in on-site research is limited. To provide an analysis of the multifaceted technological activity, I rely mostly on interviews with some of the most active members of the community (both in person in farms and via video call), rich multimedia sources from the platform and my attendance of two events. A "slow tools" summit sponsored by Farm Hack and a build workshop for a machine developed by community members. This section is structured narratively in the opposite way of the previous one. Meaning that instead of using specific events to talk about the overall activity of the community, I present the general model and providing details from my field work in appropriate points.

Contrary to L'Atelier Paysan, its role as a technology development organisation is more as a facilitator and communication hub for dispersed activity and less an active participant in the creation of new technological artefacts. As briefly discussed in the section presenting Farm Hack as a social movement organisation, its operational activity can be separated into two main categories. The Farm Hack events, which are organised throughout the world, but primarily in the USA, and the Farm Hack platform, which facilitates the cataloguing of agricultural technology and the online collaboration-coordination of farmers in the pursuit of developing new technologies.

6.1.2.1 Farm Hack Events

Farm Hack events are the points for physical aggregation of the Farm Hack community. They provide an opportunity to share prototype designs, ideas or stories and create solutions to local farmer problems by drawing on know-how available in the community. They also serve to recruit new community members, train them in the Farm Hack processes and endorse future tool development and documentation. Last, they enable organisational and individual collaborations to form as well as strengthen relationships between organisational partners and Farm Hack.

The methodology of these events evolved naturally over time. "The most successful events were the ones that were the least formal", says Dorn, while Kristen points out that they were mostly crucial for bringing people together. She continues, "Farmers have already been doing this, we're not inventing a new strategy for farm inventions or even the sharing of ideas related to farm technology. It's really just enhancing the ability to share that information". On their evolution, Severine notes that "at first they were more focused on 'show and tell'. Then some brainstorming, design charrettes. Then we did some that were more focused on a specific tool". The concept of charrettes refers to intense collaborative meetings of designers in order to tackle a specific design problem. While the term is usually employed in architecture applications, here it signifies the brainstorming session which takes place after a list of agricultural issues is identified. Typically, this process would make some people excited according to Dorn and build momentum to continue working on certain ideas. So, they started to incorporate build elements. As the community matured, "we realised there is a huge range of skills, so we made skills demos as well", he adds.

Over time, the events formulated a strong network of collaborators and gained significant traction. However, the organisational structure was under debate amongst those most actively involved in the initiative. The greenhorns and the National Young Farmers Coalition (the main organisations supporting Farm Hack), spearheaded by Severine, "wanted to direct Farm Hack in a particular direction that many of the other people involved were not interested in, so Farm Hack ended up creating its own non-profit and became independent" according to interviewee B who says it concerned how Farm Hack was to be organised: "it was about central organisation and control by a small group of people versus community oriented development, development guided by the community itself". Dorn points out at that this transpired when "at some point it became clear that this can scale up and one option was to build an organisation with support staff and regional chapters to facilitate this".

Severine reaffirms this assertion. She believes that Farm Hack lacked a "good governance structure" with the coordinative capacity to support the network. "What Farm Hack needs is few dedicated people to build institutional support", she says in order for the momentum to be maintained. They would also need to form partnerships with other organisations to secure the necessary resources to support their activity. This vision, which seems similar to the model of L'Atelier Paysan, certainly set good foundations. According to interviewee B, the way the greenhorns and the National Young Farmers Coalition organised the events was "a great launching place and have legitimated Farm Hack in a huge way". Dorn confirms that "a lot of those intensive events relied on the backing of these organisations".

However, scaling with this approach was not desired by many. Dorn echoes this sentiment: "We have plenty of competence to build a well-funded, centralised non-profit but we didn't do that, it was a conscious choice… how do you go global with that, it becomes a massive organisation". On the same note, Kristen finds that organisation like L'Atelier Paysan can bring impressive results noting how they gather significant funds but still manage to stay autonomous. "In the USA you really need to invest hard in fund raising which definitely changes the nature and spirit of the work", she says, however, continuing "I really would love to have that level of functionality but I don't think we're the same thing and so that wouldn't necessarily work for us".

They were also cautious of other forms of raising income like bringing on sponsors or selling kits like public lab. Public lab is another USA-based community creating open source hardware. They mostly focus on enabling citizens to tackle environmental concerns through inexpensive and self-made tools. There is a lot of overlap and communication between the two communities with some of the most active Farm Hack members, originally being public lab members. Public lab was "selling quasi-scientific equipment that didn't quite work as the real thing", Dorn points out. Don, who has worked with both communities on sensor applications but now is mostly active with Farm Hack, agrees with that assessment finding that effective advocacy was placed over instrument accuracy and utility in the face of very pressing issues. However "this muddied what they were trying to accomplish as an open source community", Dorn says. The message was "we're coming in this as a participant to build something that will work better but only if you participate. But that got lost because of the commerce approach which they used to raise funds for staff etc". Farm Hack does not engage in that activity, and they do not receive grants that would require that type of investments. Instead Dorn says, "We had enough volunteer enthusiasm that our efforts—investing in each other and our skills seemed a lot more fun and easier to do... the whole thing was user generated, there was no budget. That was part of the point of it". He elaborates on their preferred alternative for scaling and moving their ideas to a wider audience: "We focus instead on building an idea and a platform which other organisations with their own infrastructure can adapt and improve".

Hence, the Farm Hack non-profit was established to carry this mission which also simplified the organisational and financial issues as both the greenhorns and the National Young Farmers Coalition had fiscal sponsors according to Kristen (though there is still communication and support). The new organisation allowed for decentralised operation on minimal resources without diluting the core values of the initiative. This however has had an impact on the output. As interviewee B puts it: "Out of that conflict emerged Farm Hack at the state you see it now, free of central authority but also not developing as quickly as it might in other situations".

Kristen expands on that further: "We are essentially a peer to peer network—that is how we decided to function. It does make progress slow but that is intentional because we are volunteers". She continues: "...things sometimes slip through the cracks. It is hard because a lot of us are farmers, especially during the farming season the organisation work tapers off and if we had a lot of momentum at that time then maybe we'll lose it". Due to that, there is an ongoing discussion on whether someone who possibly isn't a farmer should be hired to do this work, but for the moment, the answer is no. As both she and interviewee B have been paid for brief periods of time for certain tasks, they find it a challenge to navigate being the only paid individual in a community of volunteers. As interviewee B puts it, "The structure of Farm Hack does not let itself have a paid employee". Dorn, expanding on this idea, thinks that after reaching a maximum number of volunteers at the early phases of the whole initiative, they received some grants to hire a couple of volunteers. That resulted in reduced volunteer activity as the paid members were expected to show the most initiative. Volunteer participation started to pick up again after paid development ended. This draws an interesting parallel with L'Atelier Paysan, and the reason with the forum is not particularly active due to, according to Fabrice, the amount of curating by the L'Atelier Paysan operational group.

Going back to the events, this change in organisational structure has had an impact on the way they were to be conducted. Kristen explains that they had to get better in partnering with other organisations and playing with their strengths to achieve common goals rather than struggle individually. To do so, they had to develop a philosophy for the events. "The idea is that Farm Hack is a banner that people can wave which was always the core to Farm Hack events—collaboration between Farm Hack and an institution like a non-profit or even a business", interviewee B explains. That idea has been expanded upon with events now organised without being curated by Farm Hack directly. The slow tools summit, supported by the "Stone Barns Center for Food and Agriculture" non-profit, was endorsed by Farm Hack to solidify such a collaboration.

Dorn, who attended the event, aims to link the output of slow tools with Farm Hack. The summit itself features farmers and small tool businesses who present their new tools and discuss ideas for new ones. While many of the participants are not even aware of the open source development process and licenses, their practices are reflective of the philosophy. Most of the time farmers make their tools to support their farming practices, as the market cannot do so, and have no desire to make a business out of them. In fact even some businesses are not particularly keen to protect their intellectual output when their main activity focuses on other products (like seeds or produce).

Again returning to the Farm Hack events, the guide for events has been developed to this end which provides an outline for what a Farm Hack event entails. People, who use the Farm Hack banner, are expected to use it and update it with their experience to figure out what works, Dorn says. A typical Farm Hack event may be facilitated by individuals (farmers), non-profit organisations or even universities, usually with minimal resources and volunteer work. They would need to be "self-funded, or locate local funding or sponsorship themselves" with connections to the local farmer community.

Documentation is emphasised across all stages of an event. The guide reiterates the goal for independent activity from community members, and documentation is mentioned multiple times. Given the lack of control over user engagement, documentation is the most important aspect of the type of activity Farm Hack engages in. As the guide puts it, "Documentation is the technology's DNA that enables it to be reproduced and adapt, evolve and hybridize with other technology so make sure that the event and the outcomes are well documented".

Several tools have emerged through these events. One of the most emblematic ones is the culticycle which was one of the first introduced. I attended one of its continuing build workshops. Events like that one are not usually publicised in the Farm Hack calendar. The reason for this, according to Dorn, is because the maximum number of people has already been reached in advance by people that already know each other and their goal. As he puts it, they "shift it from an open design event into build events or very specific design questions that the gathered people want to work on... so it goes from completely open to a bit closed". They have discussed how they could completely open up such events, but it requires a lot of work and they lack the infrastructure to manage it, which he thinks is a shortcoming and partly the reason they invite other organisations to take up certain activities.

The concept of the culticycle was introduced by Tim after he came into the realisation that small-scale agriculture does not require the horse power of even the smallest tractor available in the market. Moreover, spending a lot of time sitting in the tractor seat may give farmers back (much like a desk job) and knee injuries. This insight, according to the Farm Hack blog, is connected to the general principle of Farm Hack, "that innovation often stems from looking critically at the way things are and the way they are always done, and synthesizing from a rich repertoire of knowledge new and old to figure out how to do things better".

So, he decided to build his own less resource intensive, pedal-powered tractor that would be suitable for the type of farming he was engaging in. He was familiarised with Farm Hack through "bikes not bombs", a non-profit that repairs used bikes and sends them to economic development project around the world, and after exploring the project further, he decided that his idea should be developed further through Farm Hack. Patenting was not a viable option for him as it would require significant resources to prove that the design is unique and "somehow miraculously based on nobody's work" as he puts it. It would also require funds to defend that patent should it be infringed upon. Developing the tool through Farm Hack provided him with plenty of feedback and ideas, both through the online platform and the events, on how to further improve it by people that have built their own versions as well as the input and diverse skillsets of those attending the build workshops.

Inspiration for the original design was drawn from a simple wheel hoe he tinkered with and the schematics of an open source cultivator. The first version of the tool used walking power, enough to do the work but was quite tiring. Pedal power was soon introduced in the design, and the basic structure was defined. Earlier iterations were created using spare parts from tractors, bikes and other vehicles. Over time and several builds, the basic structure became modular and modified with a focus towards standardisation and universalisation of materials shape and size. Also, improvements were made to improve its robustness and functionality. The various versions of the tool are generally named according to the location they were built.

A toolbar is being developed with various configurations created by other members, like a flame weeder, a seeder and so on. The idea is to also standardise the toolbar as well which is mounted underneath the culticycle to conduct each farming task adding to the modularity of the design. Interoperability of the various Farm Hack tools has reached such a level that it includes modern desktop fabrication technologies. For instance, another member has designed 3D-printed rollers (components containing and distributing the seed) to be used with a type of seeder which can be attached to the culticycle. While yet another member developed a piece of software which can be used to create customised versions of the roller (i.e., changing the size, depth, shape, number and offset of seeds).

Documentation for the tool evolved accordingly. Originally, Tim created sketches and took photographs in order to track the development process. One of these photographs led to the connection with Farm Hack. After Tim uploaded the design in the Farm Hack platform, documentation became more systematic with detailed pictures and videos explaining the construction process since he lacks the knowledge to use CAD software. To make this type of documentation accessible to other users, he considered how to best combine images and text using simpler software. CAD files were created and added in later stages after Tim's design was recreated by other members of the Farm Hack community.

The gathering I attended took place in the bikes not bombs headquarters in Boston. The people present had participated in previous workshops so they were already familiar with the culticycle. There were also a couple attendees via VoIP, one of which is Michael. Michael, a former computer engineer, is a farmer-engineer who creates and sells tools and carts for small-scale farming. He encountered Farm Hack in the slow tools summit and quickly embraced the Farm Hack philosophy. Up until that point, he never considered patenting his tools or the licencing matter in general but did not consider sharing designs and information openly either. Eager to exchange knowledge and know-how, he joined the event and shared his design approach which uses wheel hub motors. The group was intrigued by his input, and he received insight from everyone else's know-how. Through this process, new ideas for further development of the culticycle collectively emerged, and individual participants acquired information and formed connections that will help them in their personal projects.

6.1.2.2 Farm Hack Platform

Plans for a Farm Hack web platform emerged early on, with its basic outline discussed in the first events and building it started soon after. Among the people attending those events were developers who were familiar with Drupal. So the decision was made to build the platform with it. The structure was similar to a simple wiki where users can create profiles and post about their tools, and gradually new features were implemented. Several core members found the earlier version of the website too technical to use and were impressed by the increased number of people using it. After the previously discussed organisational changes, it became clear that for Farm Hack's activity to be more independent and managed by the community, the platform would need to become more user-friendly and almost intuitive, otherwise farmers would not use it Kristen points out.

To improve the platform's functionality, a grant was received by SARE, the sustainable agriculture research and education programme of the US Department of Agriculture, in collaboration with the University of Vermont where Chris Callahan works as an assistant extension professor of agricultural engineering. Chris is an active member of the Farm Hack community contributing tools he has collaboratively created with farmers. The grant would not only improve the platform for its users but would also be used to better document and disseminate other tool innovation projects funded by SARE, which, by that point, were featured in a (not user-friendly) PDF database on the SARE website.

The direction of the updating was decided upon through surveys conducted with Farm Hack users and other SARE grantees. Changes were made to make the platform smart phone and tablet friendly, and the event calendar was updated for easier accessibility. The most important updates, however, have been made in the tool aspect of the platform. This streamlined process is designed to tackle the problem of limited documentation by enabling users to record their information on a tool according to their resources and time. This can be interpreted as Farm Hack's approach to systematise, as much as possible, the rich and highly diverse tool development processes taking place in the community that are poorly documented or potentially not documented at all.

According to Dorn, this is their agile approach to developing the platform that extends beyond tool documentation. He says, "With the Farm Hack platform we're attempting to express our social system. The way we prioritise tools and what people post is an expression of what the community believes is important and useful. It's an iterative process, we didn't come up with a list of what it looks like". In this sense, most of the content, like the event guide, is editable. The point is to put everything up in real time, whether it works or not, and expect the community to help make it better. Otherwise, there would be the assumption that they are providing a service rather than something for everyone to work on. This approach is reflective of the Farm Hack's general philosophy regarding technology. While technological artefact commerce is not frowned upon, the goal is "to shift that mentality and have more empowerment at the farmer level" he adds, to feel like they are building something together. To enable farmers to acquire the skills and knowledge to build tools themselves or in collaboration with someone in the community and most importantly to document it for others to learn and benefit from.

Having said that, the platform does feature an "open shops" function. This commerce section is under development, but they are being careful not to push it too fast to make sure that they are providing solutions first and then featuring resources like components and locating the relevant skills. They have had offers to sponsor certain component suppliers, Dorn says, but they have rejected them because while they do wish to enable commercial activity, they do not want to promote specific ones. To begin with, through this function farmers and other organisations or local fabricators may construct certain tools or parts which are featured in the Farm Hack library. They may also offer their services to teach others certain skills or help them build their own tools.

The tool library does not feature only schematics for ready to build machinery or even commercial products made available by community members for those that are unable to recreate them on their own (under the condition that open source licences are used). These may be proto-types under development like the culticycle or the Fido, a data (like temperature and humidity) measuring system that notifies farmers about problems in their greenhouses through text messages. The project was brainstormed in the early Farm Hack events and was taken up by three Farm Hack members to be developed. The tool was conceptu-alised as a much cheaper way to measure conditions in greenhouses located in remote locations where an internet or phone connection, usually required by commercial monitors, could not reach. So they used an Arduino microcontroller, a mobile phone and some soldering instead. To proceed with the prototyping, they applied and received some small support from the SARE programme as well. After extended experimentation and testing, the full documentation for the tool was posted in the platform. However, that was not the end of the prototyp-ing process as a new iteration using Wi-Fi signal instead of cellular began development in parallel, for when Wi-Fi is available and solder-ing skills are not.

The tools may also be do-it-yourself fixes or hacks. After all, limited resources mean there is more improvising and repurposing material, hack-ing and adapting older equipment. As several Farm Hack members have pointed out, their situation in the USA feels like going "back to the point where farm technology took a turn towards the conventional farming we know today and give it a different trajectory rather than simply use that old technology" in Tim's words. One prominent example of this is the Allis Chalmers G. A small tractor whose production ended more than six decades ago, the G is still used by many farmers to this day due to its sim-plistic mechanical system which allows for easy repairing and tinkering. Farmers have been sourcing parts and implements for these tractors from wherever they can be found (auctions, scrap yards, even Craigslist). Kristen says that they have adapted such an old tractor to cultivate in her own farm while others, like interviewee C, have converted the tractor from diesel to electric power. Farm Hack has enabled the wider dissemination of these hacks and improvements as well as the exchange of information regarding resources.

Due to this activity, small farming companies have been developing new versions of the G to cater for the demand. One specific company, which employs an open system design, has been in communication with Farm Hack. This approach allows for connectivity of components created by various manufacturers, using "off the shelf" parts and standards, rather than producing exclusive-proprietary parts that add complexity and costs. Essentially, the company has built a base power system, which can then be sourced out to other companies and individuals to use in compiling a tractor using generic parts or in any type of machinery they wish. The potential synergy between the company and the Farm Hack community is obvious as farmers would be able to acquire an affordable and easy to repair tractor while the company would receive feedback and tap into the knowledge produced by the users (adapting the farmer-designed implements into the tractor).

Carrying on with the tool library, a tool may further be a concept design, a process or even an idea submitted for collective brainstorming. For instance, farmers with a specific problem put up a request for potentially existing solutions or propose a certain solution which others in the community might help them develop further. It may also be a call for supporters in the prototyping of a new tool. For example, one of interviewee A's future projects is a versatile, scalable, low-cost, mechanical weeder (such a tool has not been produced in the USA for the past few decades due to the proliferation of herbicides). Hence, the project was posted on the platform as a call for the community to crowdfund the prototyping process.

In a similar vein, the Farm Hack platform itself is a tool featured in the library whereby users are invited to participate in its further development and content enrichment. FarmOS is another open source platform co-developed by Farm Hack members. It provides farmers with tools for mapping and planning in their farms and record keeping, like harvests and soil–water–temperature measures to increase soil health as well as crop and animal welfare. Farmers are in control of their own data as opposed to other similar services, which aggregate and capitalise on user data. This makes farm data easier to share and control in an effort to improve the tools used. It can be viewed as the Farm Hack equivalent concerning virtual farm tools that function in complementarity with the physical tools of Farm Hack, like for instance sensors and applications for data gathering and transmission. This illustrates the desire for a systemic approach to agricultural technology not driven by profit maximisation motives.

6.2   Social Construction Analysis

Having broadly presented the way technology is developed and disseminated in either case, I use the constructivist tools to provide a systematised view of this multifaceted activity and examine how these tools are being adapted in the context of peer produced, open source technology starting with the concept of the technological frame.

6.2.1   Technological Action Frame

Chapter 4 outlined the movement's collective action frame. Chapter 5 provided an overview of technological frames within the SCOT tradition as well as its appropriation in organisation studies mostly associated with ICT companies and computerisation movements. This section employs an amalgamation of these approaches into the technological action frame of the movement. As such, this frame is not only the binding material that maintains and limits the technology development network in either case or the shared beliefs and understandings on the adoption and function of the technology the movement promotes. This frame also guides the development trajectory of the technology according to the elements of the collective action frame.

The previous section of this chapter provided multiple examples of how the collective action frame is translated into a technological action frame following clues from its three distinct streams, namely the open source, peasant and organic master frames. I now condense how these frames mobilise people to adopt certain technological processes and behaviours but also shape the technological artefacts themselves.

It is obvious that technology produced is made available to everyone through open licenses as per the open source frame. Yet this expands to the design of the tools as well. Modularity and interoperability are sought after to allow users to alternate between components in the same machine or use different parts and machines in combination. The development of an ecosystem of complementary tools and approaches is desired to tackle specific types of agriculture systematically, like for instance the various tools developed by others that are adapted to fit into the culticycle's toolbar. Furthermore, new technological artefacts usually use knowledge developed by others in an adapted or improved manner, much like free and open source software forking (the process of copying a piece of software code and developing it independently).

Moreover, a significant portion of the technological artefacts are conceptualised and created collaboratively and often remotely with individuals contributing to the further development of components or updated iterations of tools. Last, in combination with the previous characteristic, stigmergy can be observed in the development of tools which is also a key characteristic of open source software (Elliott 2006). Stigmergic behaviour, observed in ants and termites, is a social mechanism in which an actor may deposit a seed, like an idea or a base project, which is then picked up by other actors who modify and develop it further into a more elaborate project. A good example of this is the 3D-printed seeder roller which was conceived independently as an idea by several individuals. The design file for the product was created by one of those individuals and was then developed further by another user who created a script which adds the capacity to alter the shape and form of the roller.

The influence of the peasant frame is also evident. Primarily, it can be found in the human-centric approach followed in the development of tools. The desire to enhance human communication through development is stated clearly in either case. Dorn says for Farm Hack: "Interpersonal relationships are important and giving members the tools to talk about what they're doing and why. And to use that in their own events and design process. That can later be expressed online but it is really about person to person interactions. That is where most of the creativity lies". Fabrice similarly says, "Sometimes I think to myself that this is a pretext to bring people together. There is something very human about the workshops, it is not just about the tools. I think this is what is most important, the collective adventure".

Technical choices, then, favour ease of reproduction, accessibility of (often repurposed) materials and reduced costs which promote communication and autonomy within the community rather than potentially embracing more complex options, which create dependencies to external inputs and expertise. This can be identified in the repurposed or retrofitted older equipment, which are given new functions. For example, see the washing machine turned salad spinner, the old bicycle parts turned into a small tractor and the old tractors and tools (decades after they have been discontinued from production) that have been given new life. It can also be seen in the focus for small-scale technological applications that enable farmers to rely on their own resources and practices for farming. Solutions influenced by the peasant frame place emphasis on the well-being of the farmer through tools that promote a healthy, scale appropriate and sustainable lifestyle, and more meaningful connections within the farmer community as well as the earth itself.

Last, the organic frame is traced in the development process as well evidenced in the efforts geared towards tools and processes suitable for small-scale, resilient-regenerative farming. Organic agriculture is not a condition for participation. Several members are even critical of certified organic practices as either not environmentally radical enough or too technocratic, rigid and expensive to accommodate the ever evolving resilient practices of farmers. However, values regarding the protection of the ecosystems and the regeneration of soil, or as one of the Farm Hack principles puts it "biology before steel and diesel", are influencing technical choices. For instance, pedal or horse power is prioritised when possible. When more power is required, electric motors are also preferred over fossil fuel alternatives. Mechanical solutions for weeding are produced, either inspired by past practices or newly conceptualised ones, over chemical ones. Similarly, holistic and system-based approaches to rejuvenating the soil rather than industrial fertilisers are preferred.

Animal welfare is another factor featured in technical choices. While both communities are invested in plant agriculture, technology for animal husbandry and holistic market gardening systems featuring animals are also devised and shared. Here, options that allow animals some comfortable living by using their natural behaviours and characteristics are considered rather than adopting profit maximisation methods designed to supress or bypass them. The mobile pigsty developed by L'Atelier Paysan is such an example as it allows pigs to have relative freedom within the farm while using their foraging and manure to revitalise the earth. The sty itself is designed to accommodate the temperature preferences of the pigs (by having enough ventilation to avoid high temperatures which pigs find uncomfortable) as well.

In practical terms, the three framings presented above are not easy to distinguish as they share several elements and are better expressed through the unified frame explored earlier. They represent the three sets of values that are combined to provide the "immaterial" components for the technology development process. The frame allows for varying configurations of components in terms of prioritising characteristics according to the values each actor deems most important.

Contradicting approaches and opinions are, of course, ever present. The level of commitment to the different elements of the frame in combination with the level of willingness for compromises create technological artefacts that might satisfy certain desires and needs (like building a tool for resilient, environmentally conscious agriculture) and ignore others (like making this tool available as a component for a diesel powered tractor). Technical choices have a wide variety, ranging from those that aspire to create tools which completely minimise externalities, in the context of an extremely resilient and autonomous paradigm established outside the (perceived as corrupt and unsustainable) dominant system, to those that seek to cleverly use this system to access the necessary resources to change it from within.

At any rate however, the communities in both cases are keenly aware of technology's impact on their activity. They critically evaluate their situation, the available resources and the options to make informed technical choices. That is, technical choices within the limits of the technological action frame.

6.2.2   Relevant Social Groups

As for social groups involved in the development process of technological artefacts, the cases are straightforward. The most important groups are those of the farmers and their technical choices over specific problems. In many instances, the technological artefact was developed solely by this group. Of secondary importance are the groups comprised by the organisations and individuals that provide technical assistance to come up with solutions for these problems or simply to systematise the solutions which would make the dissemination to others easier. In any case, the shape of the artefacts is defined less by the opposing visions of the social groups or their differing definitions of problems-solutions and more by a problematique, set by one social group (that of the farmers) and the aligning interests under a shared set of values expressed in the technology action frame explored above.

There are significant differences in the technology development processes of either case. L'Atelier Paysan employs a straightforward model. The coop's operational group is the social group in the centre of most, if not all, activity. However, their capacity to produce novel technological artefacts is determined by farmers' groups and restricted by the coop's mission (articulated by the community that created and sustains it). They provide technical skills and design know-how to assist other social groups to create technological solutions. These may be either groups of individual farmers working in similar agricultural activity or farmer associations (in some rare instances, they may be other organisations and individuals which have been inspired by L'Atelier Paysan to create their own tools which are then promoted in the L'Atelier Paysan tool list). The L'Atelier Paysan group initiates and facilitates the process at every stage. Nevertheless, it is the other social group involved, no matter what its structure might be, that is determining what the shape and function of the technological solution will be.

The same condition applies to solutions produced by farmers which then L'Atelier Paysan will document and disseminate. Only certain technical types of solutions are selected, and when adjustments are made, they follow the same set of principles. These are, again, curated in accordance to the ethos and values of the cooperative, that is, those of the farmer social group. Essentially the L'Atelier Paysan group functions as design guides or "Sherpas" providing certain skillsets, like software-assisted 3D design or engineering and architecture know-how, to enable farmers to apply their own knowledge in the creation of artefacts.

In the early days of L'Atelier Paysan, those providing these skillsets were mostly young people, fresh out of universities, seeking work experience through paid volunteer programmes. As such, they needed to be properly familiarised with the intricacies of this type of agriculture and farming technology. For this, they had to rely on their experienced peers in L'Atelier Paysan and the farmer groups they were working with. Over time, L'Atelier Paysan has acquired the resources to also employ individuals with more specialised and diverse skillsets regarding agricultural technology, which contributes to the development of more sophisticated tools.

Despite its simplistic network of actors, the community is open, if not welcoming, to input by other social groups. The coop tends to prefer giving out shares that represent groups rather than individuals. These need not necessarily be agricultural groups. They may be other socially aware groups that find the activity of L'Atelier Paysan worthy of support. One such group is the Cigales. A social investment federation with clubs (chapters) all over France which provides funds for initiatives that promote sustainable development and localised alternative models of production. Several clubs have recently joined the shareholders in L'Atelier Paysan. I met three elderly gentlemen representing one such club who offered to give me rides to the L'Atelier Paysan gathering location. Their justification for joining L'Atelier Paysan was that their group is very critical of unsustainable modern farming methods and machinery available in the market while it deems L'Atelier Paysan's social innovation model worthy of support and expansion.

In the presentation area of the gathering, two farmer groups presented their respective collaboratively developed tools. One received assistance by L'Atelier Paysan to improve certain elements of the tool. The other was independent with a strong focus on autonomy. During the discussion, which was about the ways they collaborate and possibly inspire other groups to engage in similar activity, a point was made, by a member of the cigales groups, to expand the notion of innovating together even further. Specifically, to include the consumers and supporting groups in the technical choices made. The reasoning was that these choices determine the form of the agricultural production system, which is tightly linked (or even synonymous) with the food systems; hence, it is imperative for all actors to be associated with the process. The L'Atelier Paysan briefing for the event condenses the outcome of discussion in the following sentence: "it would therefore be necessary to create spaces for design with more people than peasants alone, for technical choices that forge viable, resilient and sustainable farming and food systems" (translated from the French language by myself). This is a nuanced interpretation of technology in society considering how, quite possibly, all participants in the discussion formulated their opinions on experience rather than the theoretical examination of technology.

The Farm Hack case boasts more diverse configurations of social groups involved in the development process which echoes the same sentiment. While many of the tools are developed by individual farmers or groups of farmers, the primary goal, as stated in the mission statement of Farm Hack, is to involve other social groups like designers, engineers and activists. As Kristen puts it, how farmers manage to work the land should be everyone's concern rather than farmers struggling alone to provide food to the world. In this sense, some of the most active members of the community are not (or are part time) farmers. They may be engineer research groups like that of MIT, which participated in the early Farm Hack events. They may be engineers like interviewee A, who work closely with farmers, or academics like Chris, who finds that his employment in the university's agricultural extension programme can produce more fruitful outcomes when working with farmers rather than through one-way technology transfer from the university to the farm. Much like L'Atelier Paysan, however, the driver of activity is the farmers themselves. In Chris's words, "the first thing for me is a demonstrated need... it does no good to have a bright idea if there is no need for it".

Interviewee A, as an engineer familiarised with Farm Hack through his farmer brother, says "If I can't get vigorous feedback by the people who might consider using the tools, then I will not do a good job", and his wish is that people would be more critical about their tools as he thinks that this would produce the right environment for further development as well as repairs of equipment. For one of his latest projects, he developed three pedal-powered tools. A thresher, a fanning mill and a bicycle-powered dehuller—flour mill. He had to become a "student" of grain processing for two years and immerse himself to create them. To do so, he worked with three farms participating in the process which provided both raw material for experimentation but also valuable feedback.

For instance, his original plan was to use electric motors for the tools. However, the farmers suggested they be human powered for varying reasons. One farm had safety concerns. Another thought that pedal power would make a good marketing narrative, and the third simply objected to the motor idea because farms might not have electricity on the site. Furthermore, they decided to develop it on standardly available lumber dimensions so that farmers could easily access and experiment with local lumber. This allowed for affordable material substitutions, adaptations and modifications.

Likewise, Chris, as part of his work in the extension programme, says that his role is "to bridge research and practice. So the open source path is good for understanding what needs are out there and what solutions". In this spirit, he has developed a hop harvester in collaboration with farmers. On the development process compared to mainstream approaches, he says, "It's totally different. I like to think it as democratisation of design. Users are invited into the process in a very intimate and collaborative way, whereas generally in the private sector approach—if you're lucky—a marketing team might have had a focus group to collect user requirements that are fed to the design team. It's a very disconnected approach". The inclusion of farmers in the process led to design choices that improved the utility, in the form of portability and robustness, as well as the capacity to manufacture and repair the machine.

On the other hand, people involved in Farm Hack recognise the limitations of involving non-farmer allies (mostly engineers and software developers) in their attempt to come up with technological solutions to their problems. While collaborations might be forged with the best of intentions, lack of first-hand farming experience and misaligned interests reduce the chances for a project to reach completion or even properly launch sometimes. Without the necessary resources, it is difficult for non-farmer groups to invest a lot of time and effort to fully comprehend the problem and ideal parameters for a solution.

Design approaches in the collaborative development between the various groups also present difficulties. Another interviewee who is both a farmer and an engineer struggled with collaborating due to his specific style of conceptualising and prototyping as well as the limited skills of others within the community to keep up and contribute significantly. On a similar note, Chris says that "in some ways it makes the job more difficult for those trained in traditional design approaches but in my experience it makes for a better solution". Interviewee C also remarks that a systems-based approach of developing tools cannot be comprehended easily by engineers lacking knowledge of the basics in agriculture. So he thinks only those passionate enough to commit to the agrarian goals, or at the very least with the necessary funds to allow them to engage full-time, are able to truly collaborate with the farmers in a meaningful way.

Severine has observed instances where designer, architect and engineer groups would join the farmer group in events, and while intense collaboration would be sparked, there would be no follow-up by the "urban dwelling open source theoretical community" as she puts it. Leaving the farmers stuck with the same problem. Though she adds that there have been cases where "beautiful friendships and bonds were made in order for projects to continue and thrive". Those were a result of a culture of commitment and not one of experimentation: "A factor in the success of open source farm technology is the relationship that farm technologists have with one another. The respect they give to the user (farmer) and the insight the user has in a situation where there's little to no money".

This is observed on the other side as well. Don, as a non-farmer member of Farm Hack, finds sustainability an important issue with this type of activity. "Certainly people designing tools for themselves is going to avoid many problems", Don says, but he admits that "increasingly, for many technologies, it is becoming hard to design all the things that are useful to use". Recalling conferences and events where there were either no farmers present or a considerable gap of understanding between farmers and developers regarding the utility of certain tools, he adds, "You get into the scenario that someone will need to design it for you or with you. So there is the question of what your relationship is to that designer". As far as he is aware, some of these designers join Farm Hack as they aspire to become farmers, hence investing their personal resources to achieve that personal goal. He says his case is a coincidence of his technical skills, his scientific interests and the usefulness (impact) of the projects for the farmers—a congruency of values and skills between those involved.

The same is observed in interviewee A's case where, despite the very limited resources for him to continue doing this work, he is still engaged when possible. Often in very unfavourable conditions. For instance, he usually works in much lower rates than those of the market, which forces him to cut corners where he can (like not heating his workshop during the winter period). It cannot be avoided though, he says, as he needs to make it cheaper for farmers to create and, more importantly, repair their equipment or else they will just buy new equipment, contributing to the unsustainability of the current system. In turn, the farmers appreciate his efforts and often offer him their surpluses of produce. A relationship which is again based on mutual understanding and support.

6.2.3   Interpretive Flexibility—Black Box or Perpetual Openness?

Having presented the frame within which technology is development in the movement as well as the social groups involved in the process, it is now time to explore the particularities of the development process. Specifically the interpretive flexibility of artefacts as they progress from conception to their potential closure. This aspect of the movement also presents interesting particularities as opposed to mainstream development processes.

As was discussed in Chap. 5, differing conceptions of problems along with varying ways to solve them among the relevant social groups lead several iterations of an artefact developed as a solution. Over time, stabilisation starts to kick in with the various versions converging according to agreement reached amongst the participating social groups. Closure comes when this brewing ends. This black box state is the ideal one, and no further changes are required or, in many cases, allowed. This black box may be literal with both physical and legal restrictions preventing any type of change to the tool—machine—artefact. The black box obscures technical specifications and all relevant information forcing end users to invest considerable effort and sometimes engage in illegal activities to "unbox" the artefact.

Hacker culture is built on this premise. Individuals altering the properties of technological artefacts to imbue them with new uses. Furthermore, free and open source software is an "immaterial" technology offered freely for users to alter and adapt as they like. More recently, microcontrollers and other open source hardware are pieces of technology that have reached certain closure before they are introduced in the market. But they offer relative flexibility regarding how they are ultimately used, especially as components in a system.

Technology within the two cases displays a similar, more prominent, irregularity. The artefacts created are often purposely embracing the interpretive flexibility at any point of development. As we have seen, that point may coincide with the conception of the tool or any stage all the way down to the "finished product". Yet even that very last stage, closure is not claimed. The cases provide several examples of this.

Like the Fido which allows for different configurations depending on the setting of each farm and the specific preferences of its users. The most prominent example however is the culticycle. An interesting contrast to Bijker's historical study of bicycle used to exemplify how closure is reached, the culticycle illustrates how closure is not desired. Tim, its main contributor in the Farm Hack community, claims that his goal is for the tool to reach certain maturity as a commercial product in order for him to make some income out of. Meaning to reach a level of guaranteed operability for its users. But, beyond that, the tool's development is never ending. New iterations, implements and overall uses for it are constantly introduced. The tool itself is the polar opposite of a black box with all of its components exposed to provide easy access for modifications and repairs.

Beyond the various iterations of the tool developed by Tim and his Farm Hack collaborators, others have appropriated the tool and differentiated it significantly. For instance, the conception of a Belgian group that uses two bicycle seats for power. And the similar yet quite different Aggrozouk, which has been co-developed by L'Atelier Paysan, adopts a very dissimilar philosophy on the sitting position on the tool. The French version employs a recumbent position, using electric assistance (as well as a solar panel) to make the tool easier to manage in larger fields, whereas the Farm Hack version uses the more traditional bike riding position which allows the rider to adjust their position according to the effort required.

There is communication and exchange of opinions amongst these groups around technical characteristics, though each one follows a different trajectory of development (with these trajectories coexisting without any competition amongst their proponents). Technical characteristics are imported from other artefacts and vice versa. For instance, the four-wheeled weeder that allows users to weed in more comfortable positions than simply crouching down. It is another tool that exists in a multitude of shapes and sizes according to the developer-user's preferences on the general conception. Some are pedal powered, other electric or simply pushed. Some employ the sitting position and others the prone one. A Farm Hack forum post catalogues the wide deviations of some of its iterations.[5] How such a variety is made possible however and why?

The hop harvester, developed by Chris in collaboration with hop farmers, offers some insight. It being a collaborative development project, works began in winter when there were no new crops to test prototypes with. Hence, they developed the design with using insight by the farmers. Hydraulic power was selected over electric because it was easier to repair and troubleshoot as well as "because variable speed control is inherent in hydraulic systems and we were not sure what speed we wanted various sub-systems to operate at" (Callahan and Darby 2014, p.4). In addition, "the structural frame was made more robust than necessary in case we found certain members had to be removed to accommodate a design change in the field" (ibid.). The conception of the artefact retains its high degree of flexibility: it allows for a considerable design margin in order for its potential fabricators to adapt it to their specific production volume and equipment configurations.

Lu's pedal-powered grain processing tools offer some further clues through the interactions with other users in the Farm Hack platform. The tool blueprints do not feature a bill of materials. The justification for this according to interviewee A is the following:

> There are so many materials substitutions and adaptations (like plywood for 1X pine) that what I recommend is printing out the instructions and then on each page of the instructions write in the materials you will use. If you plan to acquire the materials all at once you can collate the pages to make a master list. This exercise will also help you get familiar with each step in case modifications you make in your design (example: substituting 3/4 "plywood for 1" pine) cause changes in dimensions and other possible changes in the instructions which will need to be pencilled in to your instructions.

Likewise, the blueprints do not feature specific instructions regarding several components (like for instance the type the bike unit used to power

---

[5] http://farmhack.org/forums/prone-weeder-lay-down-weeder-bed-weeder-collection-ideas.

the tools) allowing the user to experiment with further development to achieve a desired utility of the tool. The design of the tools has a built-in indetermination to allow for user preference (and material availability) which may affect their final form. Yet another example of preferred flexibility which also conforms to the values represented by the collective action frame.

So, the various iterations of artefacts can be developed concurrently. However, many of those may exist in obscurity. A lot of innovation in the form of different technical choices is created but not disseminated in both communities according to the interviewees in either side. The core team of Farm Hack believes that lack of time and resources limit farmers' capacity to do so. This is the reason why Farm Hack has developed educational resources and web tools, which endorse a documentation culture and simplify the production of high-quality blueprints of tools within the community.

Similarly, in the case of L'Atelier Paysan, which employs a more structured research and development model, only some of the tools in their list catalogue various version. Usually, the latest one produced by the operational group is the one featured as to keep track of all the versions would require significantly more time and resources. The community itself lacks the drive to participate in this aspect. Still, while the true breadth of maintained interpretive flexibility cannot be determined, this section illustrates how the perceived natural evolution of technological artefacts into closure is deliberately overcome in the context of alternative technologies. In Julien's words, "Even if there is consensus on the technology it can always be improved and tailored to the particular needs of local farmers. We always encourage those farmers to give back their modifications so everybody can take advantage of them".

6.3   CRITICAL CONSIDERATIONS

Broadening the scope on the bird's-eye view, beyond the interactions amongst those social groups involved in the development process, I explore the structural consideration affecting the two cases. The first section of this chapter pinpointed the various societal forces or the underlying technical technological rationale as manifested in the technical codes. It also pointed to the biased social structures enforcing limitations and standards which contradict the values and principles of these endeavours. Building on those cues, I provide a systematised account of these factors which will benefit from the, in some aspects, distinct contrasts between the USA and France contexts. To do so, I use the critical theory rubric starting with those technical codes that are in conflict with those values the technological action frame seeks to solidify as the new codes.

6.3.1   Technical Codes

Clues of technical codes having a direct impact on the cases' technology development can be found all over the previous section. Technical codes that either completely exclude users or trap them in a technological system whose values directly oppose their own. Given that the incumbent underlying technological culture is fairly universal, at least as far as agriculture is concerned, clear parallel lines can be drawn between the two cases.

The most prominent theme is the treatment of environmental considerations as externalities, which are not accounted in modern agricultural systems. Technical codes embedded in the dominant processes lead to a harmful and wasteful impact on the environment. The definition of efficiency and resilience for individuals in these cases, on the other hand, contains explicit goals for environmental sustainability if not regeneration. In this sense, the technological artefacts created by the groups are at constant odds regarding interoperability and compatibility at a systemic level. As discussed earlier, this leads to attempts to establish an alternative agricultural system and the leveraging and repurposing of existing infrastructure for their own goals.

An illustration of the latter is the use of standardised basic material, generic manufacturing equipment as well as parts, components and certain basic tools. All of which are mass produced (and are therefore deemed external inputs) in often questionable conditions. A significant concession for those determined to achieve autonomy in terms of dependence for material and infrastructure in a globally interconnected world. At this point, it cannot be avoided according to interviewee A. He says, "Right now we are not ready for how expensive life would be without mass production". For instance, while making any size of metal can potentially be made by a blacksmith, this option would not be available or affordable for many. Owning the land and having the capacity to decide what to do with it is the focus of the struggle for autonomy now he thinks. Julien from L'Atelier Paysan also believes that some tools like the tractor are too complex for farmers to build themselves, so large enterprises need to build them. Yet he believes that they too should be cooperatives owned by the workers, and they should be serving social goals rather than making profits.

Hence, the idea is to use mass production until the point of the "farm factory interface" as interviewee A puts it, meaning a garage, a workshop or a farmer's shop. There, the basic elements of technological artefacts (including the mass-produced ones) are arranged or re-contextualised in the social world to match the environmental conditions and demands of each area and the values-ethical considerations of farmers rather than attempting to solve unique problems with the mass production model. Which, he says, "is to make a million of the same tool for every farmer".

This leads to another point of incongruity with the dominant system. Proprietary configurations of technologies that, one the one hand, push farmers to purchase specific tools and implements and, on the other, prohibit them from appropriating or adapting them as they wish. This situation forces them into a vicious cycle of having to constantly upgrade in the latest version of marketed machinery or risk compatibility issues. Expensive and time-consuming repairs along with relatively cheap and disposable replacements of equipment contribute to this condition. A clear case of planned obsolescence for artefacts by manufacturers. The outcome of this is unwilling reliance on manufacturing companies and wasteful practices. To counter the effect, these groups design holistic and system-based approaches concerning their technological artefacts, which are instead aiming to achieve robustness (for long-term use) and ease of reparability. Those professionals (like interviewee A and Tim) willing to provide assistance with this process are forced to extreme measures in order for it to make economic sense. After all, adopting a research and development model similar to that of for-profit large companies is not an option.

Last, there are technical and legal specifications enforced by the state on behalf, as is perceived by those in these groups, of big companies. These specifications, designed to facilitate industrial and market interests, make alternative practices difficult or impossible to create either by providing incentives for adopting conventional practices or by applying restrictions, which independent initiatives simply cannot comply with. The wider right to repair movement in the USA has been sparked through agriculture and is in direct opposition to these restrictions. Restrictions that even question the very definition of ownership of the tool the farmers have purchased. Similar restrictions through legislations and incentives are found in the French case as well. Fabrice says they wish to introduce a public debate on the tool sector "as there is a lot of support for the private industry and we wish to question this system". As an example, he mentions that purchases of new tools are considered tax deductible. The same does not apply when they build their own tool or when they invest funds for the maintenance of their existing ones.

The previous examples have shown that profit maximisation and control of the farmers are the key values embedded in the conventional agriculture technological regime. They are realised by removing them from the development process of technology that contributes to their deskilling. As many interviewees have noted, conventional farming is now like a "desk job", in the sense that farmers are not actively engaging with the land but rather sit behind a wheel as passive users-consumers of the technology they are being fed. Worse still, some point to the trend of highly automated machines that will completely remove humans from the fields. Others might embrace these technologies but only on condition that they are there for menial and repetitive tasks which will improve the farming experience. Though they fear it is not currently the case. The connection with the soil is severed, and the instruments to care for it are set aside and replaced with those that exploit it. However, unlike other industries where deskilling of workers has taken hold and become the norm, many farmers have either retained their traditions regarding technological expertise and skills or at least leveraged the global knowledge around agriculture to re-imbue their values in the way they do their work.

6.3.2 The Role of the State, the Economic System and National Culture

Feenberg, in his otherwise extensive analysis of technology in society, (2002) tends to gloss over the massive power asymmetries between capitalist and alternative technologies as well as the role of the state in this equation. While the potential of social movements and alternative technologies to induce systemic change should not be underestimated, the opponent they are pitted against is in a vantage position. Capitalist technologies are embedded within the economic system and enjoy an abundance of resources, whereas the alternative ones operate in intense precarity and antagonistic conditions. Thus, the role of the state could be crucial in their development. These asymmetries are obvious in the case of agricultural technologies as numerous studies have illustrated their adverse effects in both social and environmental contexts. The two cases provide insights in this regard. The socio-political environment is different between the

USA and France affecting the development of alternative technologies in both subtle and less so way.

Starting with L'Atelier Paysan, the national context of France influences and even shapes, to a large degree, the community's activity. While the state predominantly provides support for conventional agriculture and market facilitated relations, L'Atelier Paysan manages to secure financial support through a mix of sources. A portion of it comes from national or European organic and small-scale farming funds. About 40% of their operations are covered this way. A significant amount indeed. The rest comes from the coop's equity and other organisations, which support their work like the cigales clubs, crowdfunding campaigns for their equipment, as well as the participation fee paid by those attending the workshops. Beside the direct support for agriculture, they manage to acquire state resources through worker vocational training in the form of tax reductions and funds for the participants. This can cover for up to 80% of the fee paid by farmers making the services L'Atelier Paysan offers both highly affordable and sustainable.

L'Atelier Paysan identify what they do as being for the public good and what they produce as commons, which they say justifies whatever state support they receive. As Julien puts it, "We are not selling machines so we cannot have the same research and development model as big companies". Nevertheless, they are aware that these conditions are heavily dependent on the political climate of the country and the situation may change. Therefore, they desire for their future activity to become more autonomous and reliant on the farmers themselves.

Indeed, political change may dramatically affect such initiatives. The Lucas plan, which was hatched in the 1970s, argued for the right to socially oriented production. It was offered as an alternative created by the employees of Lucas Aerospace under the threat of shutting down manufacturing. The plan sparked an entire movement that questioned the determinism of technology and called for the participatory development of socially and environmentally conscious technology. A leftist local government in the then Greater London Council provided resources and infrastructure for the Technology Networks, early versions of makerspaces with community-managed tools (Smith 2014). However, the hostile neoliberal policies of the Thatcher government as well as the abolishment of the council striped their resources and all the spaces from the movement (ibid). So, shielding against shifting political climates is an imperative for initiatives like L'Atelier Paysan.

At any rate, the importance of this multifaceted support cannot be understated. The L'Atelier Paysan coop acquires enough resources to employ individuals providing the required assistance full time as well as invest on other activities that actively promote the interests of these farmers and enhance their alternative practices. These individuals are either seasoned experts on the field or young practitioners, who have the luxury to fully comprehend the agricultural problems they are called to help solve as well as the philosophy and values of the farmers. French farmers, on the other hand, have access to reliable assistance with the development of tools tailored to their unique practices without having to invest excessive personal resources. Further, they enjoy all the benefits a welfare state can offer, however limited those may be compared to the privileges powerful actors and industries enjoy. Healthcare, life insurance and other state subsidies that allow them to have the time (they are even exploring ways to help farmers when they wish to take some time away from their farm activities), the resources and the appropriate disposition to engage in activities other than those that directly provide their livelihood.

Last, while France has been at the forefront of large-scale and industrialised agriculture, small-scale farmers have managed to retain the agrarian ethic and culture of the past through the many associations and organisations that promote small-scale and organic practices. The peasant identity, which comes with a sense of long history to uphold, has led to a radical perception of technology tied to autonomy, cooperation and collective action. As well as an aversion towards market relations (at least in the production aspect of agriculture) stemming from critiques towards globalisation and large agribusiness. Furthermore, artisan (the French term closely associated with that of craft) work and the culture associated with it are considered valuable in the society especially regarding food and the peasant culture. Hence, there is a market for the artisanal bread, cheese and other products (which are considered healthier, tastier and better for the environment) as well as a touristic appeal for that way of living and producing. It is so appealing that many young city people become disillusioned with their way of life and decide to become néoruraux (neorurals). I met some of those in the L'Atelier Paysan events as they were eager to acquire the skills and knowledge to become sustainable in their new role.

According to some of the people I talked to, the above provides a possible explanation for why the French farmers in the L'Atelier Paysan community are so keen to invest the time and energy to learn how to produce and maintain their tools instead of seeking someone to manufacture for them. However, some also say that L'Atelier Paysan's success may also explain why individual initiative is limited outside the umbrella of L'Atelier Paysan. Or, at least, there is limited documentation and dissemination of such activity. Since the organisation is so meticulously structured and oversees most of the development and outreach processes, many of the people in the community may not feel that their independent efforts are not required for the movement to continue thriving.

The Farm Hack organisation sets out to accomplish the same goals as L'Atelier Paysan but in a very different political, economic and cultural setting. So naturally, this setting does influence its activity in distinct ways. Agriculture in the USA is much more geared towards large-scale, energy and input-intensive practices. The sector is heavily consolidated and the market often does not offer basic machinery suitable for alternative practices, which are imported from Europe. In interviewee C's words, "I think that the capital tends to aggregate with regards to technology development. That aggregations is deployed towards technology that is applicable to industrialised agriculture. There are no incentives for small alternatives because the market is small". Those engaging in small-scale agriculture often do so in precarious conditions. The term resilient agriculture used by Farm Hack carries a connotation that goes beyond strictly about the crops. It refers to the "bounce back" and adaptive spirit of farmers in adverse situations.

As an organisation, Farm Hack receives no steady funding beside a couple of SARE grants to develop the web platform and to fund two volunteers (Kristen and interviewee B) for a year. Beyond that, it relies almost completely on the volunteer work of individuals and associated groups. The form of the organisation, the technology development model and the community events are partly shaped by this fact. Activity is quite decentralised and sporadic due to lack of funds for fully employed people to build certain decision-making institutions and coordinative capacity. Action then appears flexibly where and when community members gather the resources and collaborators to mobilise without any central coordination. A lot of individual activity takes places also. The platform is designed to facilitate that type of organisation. It provides the necessary framework, information and know-how for users to take into consideration when acting within the community. It also provides a conduit for remote collaboration, in a decentralised and asynchronous way, and the database for all the technology produced within the community. In this regard, Farm Hack embodies the full definition of a peer to peer, open source organisation.

The actions of the individuals within the community are similarly influ-enced by the local context. Industrialised agriculture has been more suc-cessful in eliminating traditional forms of agriculture in the USA. Small-scale farms are re-emerging but in a very different political landscape. Several people I talked with have mentioned the feeling of disconnection from the agricultural roots. "The small farm never went away in Europe", Kristen says, while "in the USA it feels like we are reinventing a lot of things". Dorn thinks that it is up to them to create a public record of all knowledge and technology to ensure that future generation will not have to duplicate the work of generations past. As is, to some degree, the case with them. They need to go back to the point when agricultural technology shifted into what it is today and re-appropriate it. Give it a new direction as they put it.

Furthermore, many farmers do not enjoy the same security as their peers in France. With minimal state support, it falls to them to secure proper healthcare and funds for educational courses and maintain their livelihood in case of unforeseen disasters. Farming is a high-risk, low-return venture after all. Within this context of conducting their day to day activities, their involvement in Farm Hack is more conditional as well or as Kristen puts it "emergency mode all the time". Activity is possible when time and resources allow it so the threshold for participation is kept to a minimum with a goal to, at least, cultivate a documentation culture for the tools people develop in their farms. "There is a lot of innovation in the farms that is isolated. It's inspiring to see what other have built", Dorn says. Still this is a time-consuming endeavour. Since there are no available resources at the moment to employ people to do it, Dorn mentions that a possible solution could be drawn from their model of using the resources of collaborating organisations. In this instance, university students looking to get some practical experience could potentially help with the documen-tation process of under-documented tools developed in the community.

Considering the general political and economic environment, activity in Farm Hack is inadvertently more liberal than France with a more prom-inent focus on the role of the individual in the whole endeavour. Nevertheless, as Don puts it, "It assumes a form of community structure that brings together diverse expertise which is not the ragged individualist farmer celebrated by American culture". The focus on autonomy through self-construction is less prominent than in L'Atelier Paysan as well, with more people willing to either employ someone else to build the tools avail-able in the platform for them or at least help them do it. Interviewee C thinks part of the reason is that many small-scale farmers are not from farming families so they lack the fundamental mechanical background and acquiring these skills is not easy. Kristen says that they may simply lack the time and resources to invest.

In general, commercial activity is more widespread in the periphery of the more dedicated Farm Hack community members than in L'Atelier Paysan, even though the goal is to shift the mentality and provide the necessary knowledge (by bringing experienced and novice farmers together) to do it themselves. It is encouraged in order for people like interviewee A and Tim, who invest significant personal resources and time, to be compensated and remain active in the long term. The quality of the work done is better when there are resources available as well. In the instances where funds were allocated through a SARE grant for the development of a tool, the prototyping process was more thorough and the documentation more detailed. That is because there were more materials to experiment with and funds to compensate certain people for their work rather than everyone volunteering whatever time they have available. But these grants are the exception rather than the rule.

Thus, commercial activity enables prototyping. Tim may sell some kits with essential parts for the culticycle (and people would complete them with local materials) to secure funding for further development. Interviewee A offers repair and maintenance services and occasionally is commissioned by farmers to help them develop tools. Interviewee C would like to develop his tools and practices further so that others could take lessons in his farm. Don would rather position himself as a "research and development guy" working with the farmers and securing sustainability through a grant or a foundation rather than selling tools (much like how the operational group of L'Atelier Paysan is supported). Occasionally, these tactics will fail and losses will occur. This is a topic which is under constant debate in the community, and no clear-cut solution has been offered given the lack of institutional support. For some, the ideal solution would be for these individuals that are more proficient and active than others to be compensated through workshops where farmers would learn how to build tools themselves (again similarly to what L'Atelier Paysan does). But so far, this has not been accomplished even though some have considered it. Part of the reason is the large geographic dispersion of members and, yet again, the general lack of time and funding.

What is obvious, however, is that these individuals are creating a small "market" which would embrace the ideals of openness and experimentation as well as sustainability within the community's ecosystem as Tim puts it (for lack of a better term). Not through competition but through collaboration and knowledge exchange. There are not enough resources and demand for that anyway they say. Instead, they are developers that have been working in this because they believe in it and they would engage full-time had they secured sustainability. So for some it might be a side project and for others a budding full-time job with all the growing pains that come with it.

Funds are not offered openly to anyone willing to engage so competition between groups and individuals is not fostered. Instead, people work together or on different parts that may interoperate in a larger system as activity grows organically (i.e., horizontally in a network rather than vertically around these organisations). For interviewee C, this type of development might not be as efficient as the industrial one but "when you operate inside constraints you oftentimes come up with a more elegant and effective solution than if you had a lot of capital to deploy".

The previous illustrate how the socio-economic context has a profound impact on the way technology is developed in the two cases. The shape and nature of the technological artefacts themselves are more often than not similar, in accordance to the technological frame. After all knowledge is exchanged despite barriers like distance, language and differing stock material specification. How the technology is developed; the output volume and the peripheral activities are quite different however.

Three general observations can be made on this alternative technological trajectory. First, that such initiatives can emerge and proliferate with minimal material resources in a system of technological development that excludes them. In Kristen's words, "To replace that system of research and product development system we have to be scrappier about it. Organise ourselves and share information using tools available to us".

Second, when institutional and state support are provided, even at an insubstantial degree and for seemingly unrelated purposes, these initiatives are allowed to redirect them into mobilising their untapped resources (alongside those that are mobilised, farmers often have both the infrastructure and know-how for self-fabrication after all) in a more effective way in the development of alternative technologies. The idea of "transvestment" can be instrumental here. That is to say, a process of reverse cooptation in which value is channelled out of capitalism and into alternative communal organisations (Gottlieb and Kleiner 2015; Bauwens et al. 2019). Through their business model, initiatives, like those presented in this book, accumulate resources from the state/market system and use them to create their tools and ecosystems in a similar way. Transvestement extracts resources from the capitalist mode of production and economy and transfers it into the alternative ones.

Third, truly democratised technology development is quite possible but complex and often messy. It is difficult to condense in some bullet points or create one-size-fits-all blueprint of practices for all sectors of activity. The unique values and other local specificities of each community engaging in technology development are to be accounted for even when potential contradictions do not allow for a streamlined and efficient (strictly economically speaking) model. Democratic participation can be achieved in all aspects of the process by not privileging certain powerful social groups with excessive control over technical choices. Instead, by allowing those working with and are mostly affected by certain technologies, it is possible to provide input which translates their interests and values in the form of the technology. Or better yet, by empowering them to engage in the activity themselves. These cases demonstrate this self-mobilised potential that is uniquely adapted in two relatively different, but similarly antagonistic, social settings. The book is an attempt to voice the diverse contemplations and concerns of those actively engaged in this endeavour. And to do so with some academic rigor and cohesive narrative structure.

Next, I look at the big picture: how the alternative technological configuration explored here may be positioned and even thrive in a socio-economic production mode that is similarly emerging from within the capitalist one.

BIBLIOGRAPHY

Bauwens, M., Kostakis, V. and Pazaitis, A. (2019) *Peer to Peer: The Commons Manifesto*, London: University of Westminster Press

Callahan, C.W. and Darby, H.M. (2014) "A Mobile Hops Harvester. User-based, Open Source Design and Shared Infrastructure in Emerging Year Agricultural Sector", *ASABE Paper No. 1833187*, St. Joseph, MI

Elliott, M. (2006) "Stigmergic Collaboration: The Evolution of Group Work", *M/C Journal*, 9(2)

Feenberg, A. (2002) *Transforming Technology: A Critical Theory Revisited*, New York: Oxford University Press

Gottlieb, B. and Kleiner, D. (2015) *Tactics for Economic Dissent*, Available at: https://vimeo.com/149135584, accessed 3 March 2018

Smith, A. (2014) "Socially Useful Production", *STEPS Working Paper 58*, Brighton: STEPS Centre

CHAPTER 7

Beyond Open Source Agriculture

Abstract This final chapter attempts to expand the idea of alternative technological trajectories beyond the scope of agriculture. Meaning technologies built not within the capitalist mode of production logic but from the emerging commons-based peer production mode. It maintains that for a genuine transition to a different mode of production, a shift into the underlying rationale of technology needs to also take place. This book is an attempt to apply this line of inquiry in agricultural technology.

Keywords Commons • Cosmolocalism • Design global manufacture local

Not since the proliferation of capitalism has there been a more challenging alternative to capitalist technological systems. Even socialist regimes imported technology and management methods that, in some aspects, were more aggressive than capitalism. For example, the Soviets employed industrial agriculture methods that mirrored the American ones (Fitzgerald 2003). The cases in this book provide insight on how democratised technological processes may look like. But what would be the conditions for this experience to be recreated elsewhere? After all, individuals in both cases indicate that their aspiration is for their activity to evolve into a global, organically developed, network of technology communities. This chapter discusses an emerging alternative mode of production, exemplified

© The Author(s) 2019   133
C. Giotitsas, *Open Source Agriculture*, Palgrave Advances in
Bioeconomy: Economics and Policies,
https://doi.org/10.1007/978-3-030-29341-3_7

by the democratised technologies of the case studies, which could provide the conditions for this goal.

The truly emancipatory potential of ICT has yet to be realised. And it may continue to be the case until it is applied in a production and organisation mode other than the capitalist-industrial one. The ICT has, however, made grassroots cooperation and information exchange possible on such a scale that it enables the emergence of new production models through its appropriation by technological communities. "Commons-based peer production", a term coined by Yochai Benkler (2006), is in tune with this potentiality, not as a directly competing mode but rather as one emerging from within capitalism. This type of production is distinguished from the capitalist mode of production because it involves distributed structures and its productive output is a commons. That is communal resources, administered by a community based on mutually agreed upon regulations and norms. The commons here are of the non-rivalrous nature (knowledge, code) whose multiple use does not deplete its value. In fact, it increases it.

While capitalism adapts and adopts distributed and open source forms as well, commons-based peer production boasts a qualitative change rather than a quantitative one. In this sense, it questions the basic mainstream economics mantra that humans seek maximum individual profit maximisation when engaging in productive activities. It also challenges the conventional organisational structures of property-based, market-regulated, hierarchical organisations.

An organisation and production system for commons-based peer production is described as "design global, manufacture local". The basic features of its framework are described in its name. It bypasses the industrial blueprint of restrictive intellectual properties and global logistics feeding into scaled economies (Kostakis et al. 2015). Instead intellectual property is openly accessible with knowledge creation produced in a global scale. Manufacturing takes place locally, often through communal infrastructures and with the specific local context under consideration. It endorses the circular economy concept and rejects the decoupling of inputs-outputs and their externalities. Thus, production is oriented towards sustainability and well-being rather than economic growth. The role of information and small-scale fabrication (both precision tools like 3D printers and laser cutters as well as more affordable traditional equipment) technologies is obvious for this configuration to be feasible.

Initiatives like the ones discussed here are interconnected in a global commons network. Digital communing enables them to exist both locally and globally—digitally and physically. In a sense, instead of scale-up, they scale-wide. By designing globally and manufacturing locally, communities and individuals exercise "cosmolocalism", as opposed the capitalist version of cosmopolitanism (Ramos 2017; Bauwens et al. 2019). The commons appear to be point of convergence for the wide variety of, seemingly dissimilar, projects. It provides a clarified political, economic and cultural space for collaboration. This is evident in the cases examined in this book as well. People I spoke to have been appropriating the commons as a strategic term to engage with other communities that may not be active in the same field as they but share similar views against the incumbent mode of production. L'Atelier Paysan and Farm Hack have a local orientation and impact while they share their intangible resources as a global digital commons. L'Atelier Paysan and Farm Hack have connected and created synergies by improving the same digital commons. They are emblematic cases of cosmolocalism, as the pin factory of Adam Smith was an emblematic case of the nascent cosmopolitan capitalism.

Nevertheless, capitalism is extremely successful at adapting and capturing common resources to lower its operational costs, so how would this emerging mode be allowed to flourish? There have been various proposals to ensure the reciprocity cycle towards the commons, both legally (like open source licenses modified to provisionally allow free use only for applications that add to the commons (Bauwens and Kostakis 2014)) and organisationally (in the form of open cooperativism that include stakeholders in all levels of management and are geared towards the common good rather than profit (Pazaitis et al. 2017)).

Taking the argument further, I posit that radical technological change (meaning the democratisation of the underlying technological base) would also be necessary. And for this to happen, we need to have a critical evaluation of the democratic deficit of contemporary technological systems as well as the development of alternative technological artefacts whose conception is based on a clearly defined set of values. Values that are different from those of efficiency and profit.

Several critical theorists of technology have highlighted that technical, beyond merely economic, elements have been incorporated in modern industrial systems to exert control over those directly working with the technology of production (Noble 1986; Beniger 1986). As Feenberg (2001, p.182) puts it, "the rights of workers must be structured into the design of production technology at the expense of control, not purchased at the expense of efficiency". In other words, the codes embedded in the technological artefacts and systems should reflect values, goals and interests that are exemplifying a substantive democratic orientation, besides the obvious argument of open source artefact design being available to everyone. Alternative conceptions of technology ought to be actively promoting democratic goals such as equality and political agency, rather than simply successfully challenging established technology within the framework of market rationalisation.

Commons-based peer production presents the capacity for such alternative technological systems as it is discussed through the cases of this book. This is due to the characteristics of this type of small-scale farming as well as the easily identified points of contention of the agricultural system it is pitted against. These farmers are not operating under the contemporary labour regime as it has been formulated over years in the capitalist industrial production model. Their interests and goals are much less fragmented than those of their peers in other productive sectors. Moreover, their awareness, regarding the underlying rationale of the technology they are being offered by the market, is heightened because they experience its consequences directly. The technical codes calcified within the market model are influential in commons-based peer production initiatives in other sectors, reducing their emancipatory power.

Farming, as conducted in these cases, is much like all professional farming today, entangled with market relations. Yet farmers have a long history of creating, maintaining, adapting and even sharing in a limited capacity their technology according to their needs and desires. The advent of high-tech, large-scale agriculture has severely limited this practice, but it did not disappear. Either by maintaining it through strong cultural ties (as in the French case) or by slowly rediscovering it (as in the USA case), farmers use the new ways to communicate and collaborate to elevate their centuries long traditions. The technical codes in the farming systems, practices and technological tools employed in both cases may be viewed as a radical reassertion of excluded values, in a much more globalised context, which can form the foundation for a substantive change in agriculture.

This is evident in the technology that exhibits certain particularities which set it apart from mainstream technology. Of particular interest are the stabilisation and closure mechanisms in the artefacts developed within the movement. While market-based technology tends to follow the trajectory observed in multiple SCOT studies, here artefacts remain purposely flexible with only temporary and conditional stabilisation. This marks a break from the theoretical conceptualisation for the development of novel technological artefacts, which may be attributed again to the core element of this research project. The interactions amongst individuals and groups are not primarily driven by profit but are built on the aforementioned set of values. These dictate that the tools need to be adaptable, easy to fix and intercompatible to match the needs and operational capacity of their users as well as provide optimal utility in a high-risk and antagonistic environment. Closure is, in this context, moot.

The technological action frame is then what guides these initiatives through adverse conditions while avoiding cooptation or loss of their radical vision. Thus, in the French case where it is, relatively, easy to secure funds, the frame ensures that the intense activity around technology development retains its strong focus on the values of the movement (openness, sustainability and autonomy). After all, as Fabrice pointed out, their organisation is a political project, not a service. The frame also informs the expansion of the development model towards horizontal, small-scale structures rather than responding to the demand for scaling in a vertical way. On the other hand, in the USA, the frame cautions against employing tactics to secure funds which dilutes the radical vision and, as Kristen put it, "changes the nature and spirit of the work". It also provides the (open, low-maintenance, distributed and collaborative) structure and the tools to continue producing alternative technology tapping onto those resources and partnerships which are, to quote Severine, based on a culture of commitment and respect in a situation where there's little to no money.

In this context, open source agriculture lies squarely within the design global, manufacture local/cosmolocalism framework. Previous research on the topic tends to gloss over the local aspect and focus primarily on the sexier global connectivity aspect. This book sheds light on the messy local manufacturing capacities as well. Developing and building a tool for specialised farming practices is not an easy task. The level of expertise amongst those involved is very wide. It may vary from "grizzled" farmers with extensive experience (both in manufacturing and farming) to "greenhorns" eager to acquire skills. When conditions are favourable (resourcewise), activity can wield impressive results. Diverse people aggregate in the same space and produce a complex piece of machinery within a brief timeframe with knowledge transfer taking place in a thoroughly organic way. It is the frame, meaning the set of values–beliefs and tacit knowledge, which informs and enables this capacity. As far as the discussion around commons-based peer production is concerned, this offers an insight regarding the adaptation of the mode in the different productive sectors and locations. The specific dynamics, idiosyncrasies and historical collective knowledge of any potential case need to be accounted for and integrated in the organisational and productive process to ensure viability and a radical output. A simplistic, one-size-fits-all viewpoint does a disservice to the suppressed, by the capitalist productive imperatives, capacities of grassroots communities.

The above may sketch out the blueprint for how a new technical base for society can be formulated, one that will allow workers at least some control over design decisions for the technology they manufacture and use. It may also show how to bridge the gaps and build solidarity amongst different social groups with different technological experiences and interests. After all, agriculture, as the most basic element of the primary sector, presents "fertile ground" to "plant the seeds" for change in the highly complex and interdependent techno-socio-economic system. The polar opposite of technical innovations introduced by more powerful actors in the advanced sectors dictating how the base is transformed. Dorn offers the example whereby if you think civilisation as a tree then agriculture is the roots and the population is the trunk. Arts and commerce are the branches, and if they break, they may regrow because the roots are intact. If the roots are attacked, then the system withers and dies. An apt metaphor for the current technoeconomic system attacking (altering) its roots with destructive consequences.

Taking a cue from Feenberg's call for the bridging of grounded empirical research and macrolevel analyses, this book looked into the structural considerations within the case study. A comparative view of the two subcases provides enough evidence for the effect of economic, political and cultural factors in the form of each organisation. These structural elements are accordingly noticeable in the technology development models affecting the way individuals cooperate to produce new artefacts as well as the intensity and distribution of activity. The role of the state more specifically seems to have a profound impact in this regard. Whenever the state tolerates this kind of fringe activity or even (primarily in the French case) supports it, then production is allowed to flourish. It struggles when obstacles are present either in the form of direct hostility towards such initiatives on a policy level or as calcified technical codes that come into conflict on a value-driven goal level.

At any rate though, farmers still manage to find ways to produce technology which allows them to sustain themselves according to their beliefs and values. Frequently, contrary to the homo economicus mantra of maximum utility and profit. This kind of behaviour cannot be explained away with the notion that technology follows certain paths according to the increase of efficiency in strict economic terms. This, as they will be quick to point out, has always been the norm in agriculture. Up until the advent of capitalist, industrialised technology anyway. At the individual and very local level, of course, many farmers managed to still maintain their independence and expertise on their way of doing their work. But it was the development of ICT that permitted larger-scale exchange of knowledge and cooperation. That is, to a degree which could now provide the capacity for a shift in the underlying technological rationale in society. Or at the very least, a vision for a potentially more democratised alternative of technology, technology that would allow its users to impart their personal values into its development towards a more sustainable and egalitarian version.

BIBLIOGRAPHY

Bauwens, M. and Kostakis, V. (2014) "From the Communism of Capital to Capital for the Commons: Towards an Open Co-operativism", *Triple C: Communication, Capitalism & Critique*, 12(1), pp. 356–361

Bauwens, M., Kostakis, V. and Pazaitis, A. (2019) *Peer to Peer: The Commons Manifesto*, London: University of Westminster Press

Beniger, J.R. (1986) *The Control Revolution: Technological and Economic Origins of the Information Society*, Cambridge, MA: Harvard University Press

Benkler, Y. (2006) *The Wealth of Networks: How Social Production Transforms Markets and Freedom*, New Haven, CT and London: Yale University Press

Feenberg, A. (2001) "Democratizing Technology: Interests, Codes, Rights", *The Journal of Ethics*, 5(2), pp. 177–195

Fitzgerald, D.K. (2003) *Every Farm a Factory*, New Haven, CT: Yale University Press

Kostakis, V., Niaros, V., Dafermos, G. and Bauwens, M. (2015) "Design Global, Manufacture Local: Exploring the Contours of an Emerging Productive Model", *Futures*, 73, pp. 126–135

Noble, D. (1986) *Forces of Production: A Social History of Industrial Automation*, New York: Oxford University Press

Pazaitis, A., Kostakis, V. and Bauwens, M. (2017) "Digital Economy and the Rise of Open Cooperativism: The Case of the Enspiral Network", *Transfer: European Review of Labour and Research*, 23(2), pp. 177–192

Ramos, J. (2017) "Cosmolocalism and the Future of Material Production", *Action Foresight*, Available at: https://actionforesight.net/cosmo-localism-and-the-futures-of-material-production/

Appendix

Table A.1 Participant interviews

Name	Organisation
Fabrice Clerc	L'Atelier Paysan
Joseph Templier	L'Atelier Paysan
Julien Reynier	L'Atelier Paysan
Nicolas Sinoir	L'Atelier Paysan
Jonas Miara	L'Atelier Paysan
Gregoire Wattine	L'Atelier Paysan
Etienne Escalier	L'Atelier Paysan
Dorn Cox	Farm Hack
Severine Von Tscharner Fleming	Farm Hack
Chris Callahan	Farm Hack
Kristen Loria	Farm Hack
Don Blair	Farm Hack
Tim Cooke	Farm Hack

Source: Author's creation

© The Author(s) 2019
C. Giotitsas, *Open Source Agriculture*, Palgrave Advances in
Bioeconomy: Economics and Policies,
https://doi.org/10.1007/978-3-030-29341-3

INDEX

© The Author(s) 2019
C. Giotitsas, *Open Source Agriculture*, Palgrave Advances in
Bioeconomy: Economics and Policies,
https://doi.org/10.1007/978-3-030-29341-3

143

Printed by Printforce, the Netherlands